30 Keys to Leadership

By Stanley E. Jensen Ph.D.

1st Printing
McMillen Publishing
A Sigler Company
515-232-6997
413 Northwestern, P.O. Box 887
Ames, Iowa 50010-0887

Library of Congress Card Number: Pending
ISBN: 1-888-223-42-1

This book is dedicated to my loving wife, Teresa, whose leadership and faithfulness is a constant source of encouragement, and to my first examples of leadership:

John W. Jensen and Myrtle L. Jensen.

ACKNOWLEDGEMENTS

Thanks to all my staff for their support. A special thanks to Teresa Jensen for typing the manuscript. This book was a team effort, as are most efforts in life!

Another great group of people deserve my thanks: the Ambassador's class at my church allows me to teach them, but they are the real teachers, leaders, coaches, and mentors to many people—including me. Their encouragement and friendship have profoundly aided me in writing this book.

GROWING EFFECTIVE LEADERSHIP

Outline of Contents

Chapter 1

Introduction

As president of Leadership Enterprises Inc. for over 15 years, I have had the privilege of working with hundreds of top leaders. Some were CEOs, some College Presidents; others were Division Heads or Executive Directors. I have worked with thousands of middle management and front line supervisor leaders. As I have worked with them, I have constantly kept my eye on what strengths and what principles these outstanding leaders practice. I watched for what leadership common denominators are shared by the best and most effective among them.

I have found that the habit of observing and learning from others is one of those common denominators. In the search I have identified thirty characteristics of an effective leader. These are classified into four groups of Key Elements. These Key Element Areas progress from the basic elements to ones that will cause an organization to thrive.

This book is a brief and practical application of these thirty leadership principles; I believe anyone who reads it will gain a great deal of insight for the leadership challenges that they face in today's organizations.

The first characteristic of an effective leader is actually found in the very structure of this book. The book is focused on "Key Elements" of leadership. The need for **focus** in the leader's life is paramount.

It is not enough to just focus on any thing. As a leader you need to focus on "key elements" or the "vital few"!

The four divisions of this book lead the leader to four key areas of leadership:

1. Key Elements of growth and vitality
2. Key Elements that can poison
3. Key Elements of enabling
4. Key Elements of thriving

Chapter 2
Anticipation Leadership

Anticipate no little dreams:
They have no power to stir one's blood and
Probably themselves will never be realized.
Ponder great dreams – Make big plans.
Paint a future that will rally hearts to action!

Stan Jensen Ph.D.

If you were able to listen to your own funeral eulogy (Tom Sawyer style), how would you like to hear yourself described?

If you were able to outline the comments that others will expound on for your own retirement dinner what will be some of the highlights of those speeches?

Professionals in landscaping and grounds management can see the future sight for a park, or garden, or golf course, or campus and anticipate what it will look like in five years. It will take a clear plan, resources, effort, and lots of care, but in five years it will look great. In that same way we need to anticipate the future landscape of our leadership.

What do you anticipate your leadership landscape will look like in the next 3-5 years?
To **anticipate** means to think, feel, act, and live in advance of others; to look forward to or to feel in advance, often with either a pleasant or a painful emotion. Do you look forward to a five-year leadership track record resulting in great gains and the closer alignment of your purpose, your actions, your culture, and your customer's needs?

The outcomes of organizations are determined by two major things:
1. Anticipation of the needs and expectations of those we serve.
2. Improvement of the Process that meet those needs and expectations.

The formula would look like this:

Anticipation + Process = Result

The degree to which we are successful is in large part due to how clear and focused our anticipation is of the future. Along with this clear anticipation is needed the constant improvement of the process. As the first part of the formula improves so will the last part, to great results!

Clear Anticipation + Effective Processes = Great Results!

*A great hockey player was asked what the secret was for his unparalleled success? His "secret" strategy can be summarized this way: he did not chase the puck, but rather he skated to where the puck was going to be...He **anticipated** where the puck would be and that knowledge led his all-star strategy.*

I recently read about a fascinating "sport" called Robotic Soccer. Just like it sounds small robot teams play this game. They have a robot league and a simulator league. The same programming logic is used for both leagues. Recently one team dominated the leagues wining all 8 games in the simulator league and 4 of its 5 games in the small-robot league. Neither this team nor any other team had ever had such success before. What was the improvement that caused the complete domination of both leagues? The answer is the addition of an anticipation algorithm. The dominant team anticipated each other's moves and thereby greatly improved their scoring percentage with coordinated moves. They also anticipated the defense of the other team reducing the blocks and again improving their scoring. The deciding factor was anticipation! We are not playing hockey or soccer, but we all are in a race. The organization that anticipates the needs of those they serve better than their competitors will likely win the race.

The organization that combines **clear anticipation** with **effective processes** will greatly improve their odds of winning the race.

Every **process** in the world has five main parts:
1. Work Force or People
2. Environment
3. Methods
4. Materials
5. Machinery

These 5 are the WE – 3Ms of process improvement. All five of these agents cause the outcomes of either good or poor results. Each can be examined as a possible way of improving what goes into our efforts as we meet the needs of those we serve.

Everyone in an organization serves someone. We all have customers. Customers are those individuals or those groups of people that we serve. We all have internal customers, i.e. those inside the organization that we serve by way of cooperation. We are interdependent; we serve each other so we can better serve the external customer. The external customer is our focus and our reason for existence. They are the ones that ultimately decide if we win or lose the race! We must anticipate their needs and expectations and then put together the best processes possible to best meet those needs and expectations.

Here is how it looks:

1. Focus on Customer Needs and Expectations

2. Anticipation + Processes = Results

3. Customer Satisfaction = ultimate measure of success!

Anticipation is the type of thing that must be tested to assure authenticity. Authentic anticipation is revealed in our actions and our results. I may say I want to be a great hockey player, but, if I continue to chase the puck when I know I should skate to where I anticipate it will be, my actions betray me.

My real purpose was to not look stupid. After all, at first I would often anticipate incorrectly and be found skating to the wrong spot. That would make me look stupid and my real agenda was to not look stupid at any cost. After all, even if I didn't become a great hockey player I could at least say I tried hard or I was working hard, even if it didn't pay off very well.

True anticipation starts us in the authentic direction of what we anticipate. Our mind and our will begin to make strides toward the goal. The process will be built and it will be improved as we authentically proceed.

Another way to envision this is as a Chain Reaction. The key to getting the Chain Reaction to work is to start at the beginning and to have all the right ingredients. Too many organizations try to short cut the process by starting with the results or in the middle somewhere. We must start at the beginning and we must then engage all the active ingredients.

Anticipate the Chain Reaction

Anticipation of Customer Needs
And Expectations

↓

Development of High Quality Processes

↓

Reduction of mistakes, rework,
Glitches, miscommunications,

↓

Improvement of Productivity

↓

Improvement of success with less cost

↓

Larger Market Share
And/Or
Improvement of Customer Satisfaction

↓

Stay in Business
Or Continued Success

↓

More opportunities for everyone

The Key

Once the Anticipated course is clear the Key is to get on the road.

We all remember the classic movie, The Wizard of Oz. In the story, Dorothy is growing up on a Kansas farm. By way of the calamities of a tornado, she is transported to the Land of Oz. In the Land of Oz she has a problem... she wants to go home. The locals advise her to go to the Emerald City and there she can see the Wizard of Oz. Perhaps he can help her get home. When she inquires about the way to the Emerald City she is told to follow the Yellow Brick Road. So what does she do? She gets on the road. She anticipates that the Wizard of Oz can help her so without over analyzing the situation she gets on the road!

A little ways down the road she meets a scarecrow. He has a problem...he has no brain! Do you have any employees or leaders that may have a similar problem? Well, Dorothy suggests he joins her and maybe the Wizard can help him too. So he too gets on the road.

The two travelers have not gone far when they find the Tin Man. His problem, as you recall, is he has no heart. Know anyone like this? The invitation is given and he too joins the team.

In the dark forest, the three adventurers meet a lion. A Cowardly Lion, and of course his problem is he has no courage. Know any leaders like this? Of course after some encouragement the Cowardly Lion decides to join the team, and their process of getting to the Emerald City. The team is filled with the anticipation of reaching their team goal as well as achieving their individual goals.

However, as with any worthy endeavor it is not long before they are confronted with unbelievable roadblocks and those in opposition to their progress. You have to admit, winged monkeys, a fortified castle, and a really scary witch are just about as formidable as some of the things that confront us at work.

Well, it turns out that the Scarecrow had a very good ability to problem solve once he was on the road to a meaningful goal with a team he cared about. The Tin Man discovered his heart as he joined a team that cared about him and his needs as they all pressed toward a goal bigger then any of them could take on alone. The Cowardly Lion discovered powerful courage that caused him to lead the attack as they took on a force ten times their number.

The key that started their success was the act of getting on the road. One researcher found that 80% of the lessons learned by leaders were learned in the act of leading. We tend to learn courage when the leadership situation demands courage.

I have built over 400 process improvement teams. Each team was built to improve a real and very important process. Teams, I have found, learn to solve process problems best by working on real and meaningful processes that they care about. Not through practice sessions where they are asked to learn the concepts as they build better paper airplanes, but in meaningful, real-life processes.

People develop heart while engaged with others in the pursuit of a goal that is meaningful. We respond to needs when we are placed in situations where authentic needs are experienced by people that we have grown to care about. Those people can be both customers and colleagues.

The chapters ahead are designed to be practical. They are short and to the point so the concepts can readily be put to use. Let's get on the road!

CHAPTER 3
IMAGE!

We are in the business of creating an image! Nearly everyone associated with our organization is responsible, in a significant way, for creating an image for our organization. People's first impression of our institution or our business or our city and our county is largely in our hands. We are image-makers!

Actually every one of us personally and corporately have no choice but to make an impression. The question is, what kind of image do we project? Are you as attractive as you would like to be? If your answer is yes, then you are in the minority or you may be in denial. All of us can work on our image as an organization and as individuals.

While working my way through grad school, I worked at United Parcel Service (UPS). One of the jobs I did while at UPS was to wash those brown trucks. We washed everyone of them every day! Why? Some days they were really not all that dirty, but we washed them everyday! The reason is *image*. For most of our customers, or potential customers, those brown trucks were the only pictures they had of UPS. Most customers built their impressions of UPS on the image that those clean trucks projected. I was not in the truck washing business. I was in the image creation business.

When people see you, your personnel, your vehicles, your grounds, and buildings what is the image they project? Some of the image at your organization you may have little or no control over. But you have a lot to say about your own personal image. Your personal attractiveness to other people is a mixture of at least three things:
1. your inner self
2. your outer self
3. your vision and dreams

With these three in mind, ask yourself the following important questions:

Your Inner Self

What is your mental position on life?

We often hear this question put this way, "What is your attitude?" The definition of attitude has to do with our mental position in regard to a fact or situation. I am in charge of my mental position or attitude about life. I may not control much of what happens in the whole scheme of life, but I do control my response to or my attitude about those things.

Do you know anyone who creates a good image when he or she is gloomy or negative? I can't think of anyone. Those with solidly positive mental positions at work are not oblivious to the problems. They see the problems, but often immediately explore possible solutions or at least have faith that they will find a solution in the future. Effective leaders *learn* to have positive attitudes!

Have you noticed that there is no direct correlation between those that have a positive attitude and being in a positive situation? Those that have great health and lots of money are often not the most positive people. Those with terrible health or perhaps little money can often be very positive people.

Christopher Reeve, the actor, upon becoming quadriplegic recalled, "On the wall of my room when I was in rehab was a picture of the space shuttle blasting off, autographed by every astronaut now at NASA. On the top of the picture it says, *"We found nothing is impossible."* That would be a great mental position for all of us to take, especially while facing the deepest struggles of our lives.

Nothing is impossible! What is your attitude?

Am I self-focused or other-focused?

One of the leadership lessons I keep learning more about is the importance of being focused on others, especially those you are trying to serve. Do I worry about what others will think of me, will they accept me, will they think I'm sharp, will they like me, will they appreciate me, will they respect me? If I am only focused on myself I will be a loser. I must realize everyone wants those things. My worrying or hoping will not get them. I can not force anyone to give them to me.

But, I can give them to others. I control only my end of the relationship. I can accept them, I can think well of them, I can find some strengths about them, I can find something to like about them, I can appreciate them, and I can respect them. As I authentically become other-focused, I can authentically become a friend. Those who would have friends must show themselves friendly.

Do I really love people?

Art DeMoss made popular the phrase, **"Love people and use things – don't love things and use people."**

Authentic love is not an easy thing. In fact, it often is the toughest thing about great leadership. It may also provide the greatest returns.

Authentic love for others is a key element in building a one-of-a-kind culture that will attract the best work force and that will delight those we serve. It is easy to return love to those that are kind to you, and it is also easy to care about those who are pleasant. It can be tough to love those who are at first rude and insulting.

The first impressions are important because people make many judgements in that first encounter. But it is a leader's *heart* that is remembered as people reflect on their place of employment.

Does my leadership encourage others?

Especially in this day and age of instant gratification and instant success, the ability to encourage is much needed and will create a magnetism that will attract both good employees and repeat customers.

Encouragement means to pour courage into…to bring renewed vision and hope. It is not hype or false hope, but a clear and realistic view of a positive future. The leader, who can see the reality of the situation and yet find enough courage for self and enough to pour into others, is on the way to great effectiveness.

Although its setting is Scotland in the 13h century, the movie Braveheart has earned kudos and box office success—including an Academy Award—the world around.

Why? Mel Gibson, the Australian-raised American who produced, directed, and starred in the movie as the Scottish leader William Wallace, told the London Observer that such stories of ancient heroism are an effort **"To raise ourselves above the normal level of things. There is a sense of something higher in all of us. I don't care who you are."**

What meaning does this hold for today's leader? The movie script provides some of the answers. After routing the opposing forces of 50,000 in the first battle of Stirling, the newly-knighted Wallace, Gibson's character, delivers this lecture on the responsibilities of rank to Robert the Bruce, whose policies as Scottish king were to set the country on its way to a new prosperity: **"What does it mean to be noble? Your title gives you claim to the throne of our country. But men don't follow titles. They follow courage! Just lead them to freedom, and they will follow you."**

Encouragement will often lower turnover. It will lead to increased productivity and it will draw out the best in people. Encouragement will help you win the race for more customer satisfaction and larger market share. Best of all encouragement helps us win big without resorting to being small.

Your Outer Self

What can I learn from others about attractive image?

In America, we may focus too much on the outward image or outward appearance. However, we need to give it enough attention so that our outer self does not detract from our effectiveness as an individual or as an organization.

Can you think of a friend or another leader who has an image that you like? If so, observe where they shop or where they get their hair done. A wise old professor of mine once reflected upon his philosophy concerning outward attractiveness. He said, **"If the barn door needs painting, paint it!"**

Does my appearance or image match my position?

We can all observe some division leaders and some CEOs that still dress like college students. Or some leaders who, in an attempt to identify with their front line crew members, still dress in jeans and tee shirts. This may result in neither impressing the crew nor in being effective with other leaders in your organization.

Never forget your roots, but don't undermine your division by under dressing for your leadership role. A principle to remember: Clothes reflect the position.

Do I have enough energy to set the right image?

Every one thinks they can cheat on their body and it will not tell, but our body needs enough rest, exercise, and the right kind of food, or it will tell everyone you are cheating and your image will pay the price.

Your Vision and Dreams

Do I have a future?

I have met 80-year-olds who are planting trees and looking forward to seeing them mature. My Dad and Mom are in their mid 70s and are currently building a new house to enjoy as they get older. They have a vision of a great future. They have a great attractiveness and a great personal image.

I have also met 17 year olds who can not envision the next weekend. Who have a vision that is summed up in these words: "Life sucks and then you die." Far too many of them are taking their life because they see no future. They are young, but very, very old at the same time because they see no future.

Having a positive future vision is very attractive and helps create a great image for you and your organization. What is your vision and what are your dreams?

Do I actually anticipate my personal appearance being one of the best investments I can make for my future?

To important people around you, your appearance makes a definite statement about who you are and what you think about yourself and your department. What kind of statement are you making?

It takes only a small amount of investment and some thoughtful time to make a relatively big improvement in your personal appearance. Concentrate on hairstyle, tie, belt, and shoes. Each of these can make a major difference in a man's appearance.

Women can focus on some of the same things. But for each gender it is important to develop a good understanding of the appropriate wardrobe for the occasion. For example: formal business attire for the board room, a business casual look for day to day office leadership roles, and casual attire for front line field leadership roles may be a good rule of thumb. Clean and neat is always appropriate.

Remember, too, that your appearance isn't a reflection of you alone. At different times it also reflects on your team, your organization, your profession, even your spouse and family.

CHAPTER 4
BALANCE

In my office hangs a Japanese Origami Mobile depicting a small flock of birds in flight. Each bird balances another as they gently glide in never ending flight. A friend bought the mobile to celebrate our achieving a long sought-after goal. She said it would serve as a constant reminder that one of the keys to success is a life of balance.

I have found that living in balance is no small achievement. Our mobile hangs near the door to my office and the traffic of entering and exiting people will often cause the flock to fly into the vortex of someone's passing wake of "wind". This disturbance can cause the birds to get tangled. Often, at the end of a day of frantic deadlines and hurried schedules, I will notice the flock is flying in a new weirdly ajar formation. It is then my task to gently work the individual parts of the flock back into a balanced formation.

Are you out of balance?

Have you ever found your own life tangled into a counter productive formation? Too often I have experienced the ravages of imbalance. It is one of the experiences of life for which I do not need another guilt-laced lecture. I know it can be damaging, the question is how to avoid the imbalance. How do we escape once the strings of our lives are tangled almost beyond hope? Better yet how do we avoid the ravages of imbalance?

For instance, you may know the elements that must be present and must be in balance to bring good growth and health to plants: sunlight, water, soil with its nutrients, the right temperatures, the right plants that compliment and don't compete, and even the right seasonal cycles. Balance in the long run brings the most health and the most fruit.

As humans, we too need some sense of balance in our lives to best grow and thrive. As leaders, it is perhaps more important to achieve balance. We affect others around us, and we are often the primary architects of the systems in which others will work and thrive. It will be tough to create balanced human systems at work if, as an individual, we don't have a clue what it means to be in balance.

When we use the word "balance", my first mental picture is of an old fashion balance scale. If we put a gram of weight on one side of the scale we have to balance it by placing a gram of material on the other side. This picture is not a good one for a multitude of reasons. One, human systems are 3 dimensional. Two, we are engaged in balancing 8–10 areas of our personal life plus the many areas at work. Three, none of these areas stand completely alone—they are all connected and they all effect one another. It is a network that we need to balance not just one element against one other element. Our lives are as complex as any ecosystem.

Do you ever get that feeling of being overwhelmed? When I have been hit by the storm of being overwhelmed I feel like a boxer in the ring, as my opponent delivers one series of blows and then another. It leaves me feeling dizzy, fatigued, and unable to anticipate when the next punch will come. I start to see problems where there are none and am completely caught off guard by actual assaults. I see myself, gloves down, half conscious, and taking a blizzard of punches. What should I do…? Answer—get out of the ring!! Pray for the bell to sound the end of the round!

When you feel you're in a blizzard of mind numbing punches, bring your schedule to a halt. Get out of the ring even if for a short half-hour break to regroup. If you can no longer focus, or your efforts have deteriorated to flailing at the wind, it is time to retreat in order to regain balance. It is time to refocus.

Investing Time – To Save Time

Some time ago I was reading a short biography of a very successful person. The reason I read these things is to gain some insight into what they did that contributed to their success. The bottom line for this leader was the habit of spending one to three hours a day just thinking. Thinking about their business, their life, their mistakes, and the best solutions to challenges they faced.

My first reaction was perhaps the same as yours…it would be nice to have so much time to spend thinking. Surely this leader was lazy, or perhaps so rich he didn't have the same pressures you and I experience. Truth is, he is a multimillionaire. But, he also spent years of his life learning from mistakes and being in the pressure cooker of financial failure. Even during those times he devoted hours each day to learning the discipline of balance and focus. He attributes his great success to those hours.

I have sought to "invest" one hour a day in staying in balance. It has paid off in many ways. I anticipate the future will hold even more returns on this investment. It takes courage to stop the race of life in order to retool or refocus. It will feel like too much time is "spent" in keeping your life in focus and balance. But if done honestly, you too will find it to be the key to long term effectiveness. Ask yourself the following questions:

Can I refocus specific areas in which I am experiencing imbalance?

We can make life too complex. Systems in organizations can be very complex as they entail hundreds of processes, with each process containing scores of parts. Still, I find these systems can be broken down to the vital few that really drive everything else. Life's vital few seem to fall into eight categories.

On a scale of 1–10, one being very unbalanced or unsatisfied and 10 being very balanced or satisfied, how would you rate each one in your life?

Spiritual Health _____
Mental Health _____
Physical Health_____
Financial Health _____
Marriage and/or Family _____
Friends_____
Vocation _____
Life Purpose and Plan _____

What are the areas that you're most satisfied with? These strengths may be used to help with the areas you are less satisfied with and aid you in bringing your life into more balance. It is especially important to be clear on your life purpose.

Why are you here? What is your life purpose?

I know this can be tough. Odds are your organization has a purpose statement. The purpose of an organization helps it make all sort of decisions. Knowing our core purpose in life will help in prioritizing how we spend our time, our money, and our energy.

Each of our resources is limited. We only have 24 hours a day. If I devote an hour to exercise, I am also deciding to not spend that hour in the office or with family. The dollar I choose to spend on entertainment is one less I choose to invest in education or in the stock market. It is easy to see how every decision can either take us toward greater balance or into greater imbalance. Every decision effects each of the eight areas of life. Which brings me to the next suggestion: memorize the eight areas and make them yours. Reword them if you would like or change the areas in some way but make them a part of our automatic thinking process as you make decisions. Your life is a connected system.

To which of the areas of life have I been giving too much time, money, energy or emphasis?

Which area(s) have I been neglecting?

It is important, at this point, to separate fruitless worry from fruitful action. Worry can use up so much energy and time that it causes us to become stuck in anxiety. The key is to work on all those things you can, no excuses. Remember, some outcomes may not be under your control.

You may identify physical health as being out of balance in your life. If you have an incurable disease, you can pray and join a support group, but it still may be that good health will never be a result you achieve. The key is to do all you can— actively control all you can—and then invest your energy in other areas. Your life can be in better balance, but it will not be perfect.

What are two or three clear and specific things you can do to correct the imbalance you have identified?

On a daily basis, here is how it might work out: you have a clear idea as to your over-all purpose in life, but every day you may need to take a short break to assess the pressures of imbalance you are feeling. So, you take a walk to think or, while on the daily commute, you talk right out loud (assuming you're in the car alone) to yourself or to God. Better yet—you stop at a park.

Think through the eight areas of your life and quickly assess the areas that are causing out of balance pressure. What can you do? Even if you can cut the lost balance by 30% with your action plan it will help get things heading toward better balance. If you focus on what you can do, you will walk away from the park an hour later with more personal balance then when you arrived.

Even with a clear life-long direction or purpose, you will need to take daily course corrections to stay on the path toward your destination. Sometimes it helps to do a little reality check. Ask these two questions:

What will be the negative result if I continue living with this imbalance or bad habit in my life?

What will be the price and the reward of becoming balanced in this area?

What will happen to your health if you keep gaining 10 pounds a year like you have for the past 5 years?
What will it take to start a new habit in eating and in exercise?
What will be the rewards in the next 5 years?
The answers help move us into reality and into action toward better balance.

At the end of her high school education, one of my sisters had the opportunity to become an exchange student in Germany. She lived with a delightful German family and attended school. One day in a conversation with the family, the father was asking some questions about how our family lived and some of the daily life aspects of life in our family. It was his habit, and that of his son, to drink and smoke quite heavily. When he discovered that my sister's father and brothers did not smoke or drink, he was surprised and declared that we must be very wealthy, being that we did not spend any money on such habits. He had counted the cost of heavy drinking and smoking. Instinctively he knew those resources could have purchased many others things.

To what areas am I devoting most of my energies?

What is the dominant preoccupation of your mind, your heart, and your spirit? Is it your family? Your career? Your friends? Making sure you are never embarrassed? Making sure others don't hurt you? Is this the way you want it to be?

What hurtles will I need to overcome in order to change?

Begin by anticipating your successful change. In your mind's eye, see yourself enjoying your new, better habit. Start to overcome the hurdles.

Who can help me and encourage me toward better life balance?

Get a friend to help, to encourage you, and to hold you accountable. Do the same for them. Iron sharpens iron. Two or more can work toward life balance more effectively. We help each other become objective. We can support, encourage, and give good advise to one another.

I have been privileged to be a personal coach to over 150 leaders. At times, I have had my own personal coach. I have almost always called on friends when I needed help overcoming difficult problems or disappointments. The coaches and friends have always aided me in making better progress.

Remember a well-balanced wheel can roll faster and experiences less wear and tear!

Chapter 5
Faith + Love = Respect

One of life's greatest pleasures is accomplishing what others say you cannot.

Nearly every effective leader is tested at many points in their leadership life. In fact, often the leader has to deflect a constant stream of challenges that can undermine confidence. They sound like this: "That will never work..." or "You can't do that..." or "You better be careful..." Real and realistic faith is needed. Faith is that uncanny ability to see things clearly before they appear.

The biggest challenge is not the outside lack of faith from others. The really tough voice is the one on the inside, the voice of self-doubt. Take some comfort in the fact that most leaders at some time have questioned their own competence.

The key is to have authentic answers for the voices of doubt. I often give keynote addresses and speak to audiences of various sizes. Not long ago, as I anticipated the opportunity to address a group of 500 Educational Leaders, the inside doubt voices started their questions. "Who am I to address this group?" "What do I think I am doing here?" "This will be a tough audience, what will they think, will I meet their needs?"

Have authentic answers for yourself and others. Here are some of mine from that day: I am a Servant Leader. I do not pretend to have all the answers but I can contribute some significant ideas that I know work. Every audience is different and this is my first introduction to these people, but I have had success before with similar types of audiences. The president hired me and I have asked a lot of questions to determine the needs of the group. I believe I am the person for this job. I have a worthy message and I care deeply for the people I am about to meet. I trust God to help me. I was made for this hour. I am making every effort to serve with excellence.

The authentic answers generate perspective and balance. They give us energy and faith to take on the most difficult of tasks with confidence. Remember to focus on the things that you control, not on the things that others control. I really care about the individuals I serve and lead. I hope they care about me too, but I don't control that. You might not be giving a keynote address, it may be that you are outlining a budget, or a new strategic plan.Whatever the challenge is, be ready to answer the inside and outside voices. Have authentic answers. Have faith and project the confidence that it gives you. Others will be attracted to your leadership.

Life without love is like a tree
Without blossom and fruit.
(Kahlil Gibran)

Effective leaders love people and have a passion for the mission they are pursuing. We all love ourselves, and this is normal. We protect ourselves. We brush our teeth. We look out for ourselves. The transformation takes place when a leader authentically looks out for his co-workers, or protects her team, or helps others become healthy.

We are attracted to a leader who has faith in us and loves us. We follow and give respect to such leaders. After all, they are giving respect to us in two of the most powerful ways: faith and love.

I have found it necessary to cooperate with, and follow, many leaders I do not respect. However, I will more gladly sacrifice and give even more to a leader I deeply respect. A friend of mine was the Director or Human Resources for a large convenience store chain. He told me one day that all the new employees he hires at the corporate headquarters are given the same orientation. Part of the orientation for each of those new employees is their introduction to the corporate values. Part of those values is his total commitment to their success even if that means seeing them promoted out of the corporation to a better position somewhere else. Wow! Do you think he lost more then the average number of people? No, people were attracted to his commitment and stayed in high numbers!

Some are certain to object to the idea that faith and love can be a realistic part of leadership today. After all, don't I know that there are lots of mean people in the world? Haven't I experienced the betrayal, lies, and political treachery that run rampant in many organizations? The answer is a big YES. In fact, recently a friend commented that he found it remarkable and inspiring to him that I was still standing after all the difficulties that I have overcome.

True care and commitment is most needed and most noticed in the midst of cynicism and betrayal. Abraham Lincoln certainly understood defeat and deep sorrow and yet he said: **"All my life I have tried to pluck a thistle and plant a flower wherever the flower would grow in thought and mind."**

Guard your heart against bitterness, its roots will contaminate your every thought and motive. It is a study in irony, to contrast how we think of a cup with a chip in it, and how we reference the Liberty Bell even though it has a distinct crack. The one we are tempted to discard if we choose to think of its wound as permanently reducing its value, while the other we choose to think of as a heroic reminder of battles won, at great cost. The key to victory over past wounds is in how we think of them. I have great respect for leaders who have the battle scars that come with leadership positions and yet still display renewed faith and love. They have roots of confidence, not bitterness. They know that we will win most leadership battles with faith and love, and their confidence is contagious.

CHAPTER 6
CREATIVITY AND LEADERSHIP

Creativity for the leader will take many forms. At its core, creativity is a combination of hard work, great questions, and looking at things in different ways. Frankly, lots of creative ideas come from looking at things in different ways because something is pressuring us to find another way. The result is creative solutions to old problems.

Have you ever been at a seminar where the facilitator instructs the participants to line up at one end of the room and make their way one by one to the other side of the room? The challenge is everyone must proceed to the other end by a different means. One at a time people must think of a different method of getting to the other end. No two ways can be the same. I have seen as many as 200 people creatively come up with 200 different ways of covering the same distance safely.

Participants usually take on the activity with some hesitation. Of course, those participants toward the end of the line experience even more of a challenge. Some insist they cannot think of any new way to traverse the distance. But, in a short time they came up with a creative method. Often, creativity is a result of pressure. It is true that **"Necessity is the mother of invention"**.

The inner motives of the participants are perhaps as varied as the solutions they created. Some became creative to avoid embarrassment, some to please the facilitator, some were just glad to be involved in an activity. For others, it was the motive of competition. We can all become creative if we know it is necessary.

The problem is we sometimes don't know we need to become creative. Sometimes we wait too long to become creative. Leaders need to anticipate changes in their organizations and become creative in solving problems before it is too late.

In one Midwest agricultural company I conducted a series of change seminaries. In each seminar, the participants were asked to envision some of the changes they will face in the next 5-10 years. One challenge that came up often was the future lack of qualified employees. Groups were charged with creatively coming up with solutions to this problem. When "forced" to generate a solution it was amazing what great ideas they presented.

Creativity happens best when there is a need for solutions but not a panicked need. Some of the most valuable ideas can come when we force ourselves to look at everyday problems in a different light.

Limitations are absolutely essential to creativity. In an interaction with limits, the creative act comes into being.
(Rollo May, *The Courage to Change*)

Here are some key questions to start with:

What are the top five problems for your industry?

What are the top five problems in your area of the organization?

Why is it important to solve these problems? (What are the benefits of solving them and what are the consequences of not solving them?)

What are the top two things holding back your personal progress?

If necessity is the mother of invention, then **necessity and limitation are the parents of creativity.**

Often, the teams I build have been challenged to create significantly better outcomes with the same or fewer resources. The emotional trail these teams followed usually goes like this:

1. Why hasn't someone solved this problem before?
2. No one else has this much of a problem.
3. We can't do this... No one can!
4. What we need is more time and more money; (this is sometimes part of the solution but lets not go there yet).
5. Can we avoid the problem? Sidestep it? Ignore it? Blame someone else?....
6. The deadline is coming, we need to come up with something or bad things will happen or good opportunities will be lost or...
7. A different look at the data and facts gives us an idea.
8. We can do this!
9. Here is the plan...
10. We did it... that wasn't so hard.

Another important consideration for improving creativity is to benchmark against what others are doing. **Be curious and ask lots of questions.**

For thousands of years, people have enjoyed hot food by one means of heating that food – fire. Yes, in relatively recent history we put a twist on electrical energy and have heated food with electric stoves and ovens. Still, those in the "heat up the food business" were under pressure to speed things up and get our food and drink hot faster, and with fewer hassles.

Finally, someone in the "heat up the food business" heard about the experiences of some soldiers that were operating one of the first radar units. Radar was being developed to detect incoming enemy aircraft and serve as an early warning system. Reportedly, the soldiers found that they could stand in front of the radar unit and get warm. The warmth was especially unusual because nothing in the unit was warm. Nothing was radiating heat like a hot surface or a hot motor.

This observation was of little interest to those seeking to detect enemy aircraft, but to those in the "heat up the food business" it was of great interest. Soon, someone in the "heat up to food business" became creative and invented the first microwave oven! They were first called "radar ranges."

The result of such creativity has radically changed how we cook. It has changed how long it takes, what dishes are used, and how we think of cooking. The discovery might never have happened if someone hadn't gotten out and looked around at what others were doing.

A + B = C   "C" is for the Creative solution!

The first and most important step toward success
Is the feeling that we can succeed.

(Nelson Boswell)

CHAPTER 7
TWO SIDES OF SELF

Self-Motivation   and   Self-Discipline

To have motive is to have a sense of need or desire. All people have needs and it follows that all of us are motivated. The motives of those around us may be completely at odds to ours. They may be out of step with the purpose of meeting the needs of our customers. But everyone is already motivated in some way.

What we mean by self-motivation is usually characterized by attributes such as being a self-starter or being able to see work and be motivated to get it done. One of the early lessons I learned from my Dad, as I grew up on our Iowa farm, was the need to see work and do that work without being told. He clearly communicated disappointment with me when I didn't see the work and didn't get it done; this was my motivation for mastering this principle sooner rather then later.

For the leader, great communication and great motivation have some parallels. The start of clear communication originates in being very clear in your own mind and heart as to what you wish to communicate. If the message you want to communicate is foggy to you, it will be dark as night to your listeners. Great motivation for others in your department or in your organization needs to start with YOU! You must be motivated! The start of effective motivation is in your heart and in your dreams for the organization.

Great communication starts with a clear message but then you need to transmit that clear message to others. We do this best by sharpening our skills of communication. Likewise, we must sharpen our skills of transferring motivation to others. What authentically lights our motivational fires? Others in our organization will likely identify with some of the same needs and be motivated by some of the same things that motivate us.

Like effective communication, effective motivation starts on the inside of the leader. I remember, not long ago, listening to the very successful leader of an insurance agency. He told of how at one point he was ready to give up his general agency. He was frustrated, discouraged, and tired of his lack of success. Today, he leads one of the most successful and most respected General Agencies in the country with over two hundred employees. Talented people even outside of the insurance field seek him out and want to work for him. I must admit that by the end of his one-hour speech I wanted to work for him. Insurance is a field filled with lots of great people and a great service, but not a vocation I had ever been attracted to before.

This General Agency CEO showed us charts demonstrating how the general public's respect for Insurance Agents is only one notch higher then the typical Used Car Salesman. So what caused people to flock to his Agency in a field that is not well respected, and that nationally experiences single digit retention rates for agents?

He didn't sell "insurance;" he and his team partnered with people to aid them in better understanding the number one, most private, and most misunderstood thing in our life—money. They dealt with personal, family and business security, how to better succeed, how to understand and get money to serve needs instead of us serving money. It was not a motivation like that of freshly poured root beer—you know, lots of frothy furry and little root beer. No, it was an authentic, quiet excitement for something he had seen work and to which he was totally committed. He knew he made a positive difference in the lives of both his customers and his team. He was self-motivated and it was contagious!

I have had the honor of serving in the Professional Grounds Management Society (PGMS). The members of this national organization are leaders who manage golf courses, college and university campuses, estates, etc.

Members of PGMS are not in the "grounds business." Their basic purpose and motivation is not to be leaders of people who mow grass, landscape, grow plants, plant flowers, nurture trees, and maintain equipment and buildings. **No, they are Image-Makers for their organizations!** They lift the spirits of people who experience their grounds. They orchestrate a better life experience, they help customers inside and outside their organization produce more and enjoy life's bounty more!

As a leader, what is your inner motive?

Noted motivational guru Peter Schultz tells the story of three people who work on the same construction site. All three workers were doing the same job, but when each was asked what that job was,, the answered varied. "Breaking rocks," the first replied. "Earning my living," the second said. "Helping to build a cathedral," said the third.

Do you have a clear understanding of what you really do?

Does it motivate you? How? Why is it important?

How does what you do change the world?

Are you authentically motivated?

What ever your answer is… yes or no…it shows! Those around you can tell.

Get clear self-motivation. Be clear about what you are doing. Be clear about the WHY of doing what you are doing. Also, it is important to begin to peel off the things in your thinking that may diminish and may undermine your motivation.

What perceptions de-motivate you? Get rid of them!

A couple years ago, I developed some Leadership Development Training Material for one of the largest agricultural companies in the world. In beginning the process of teaching the material I was working with over a hundred of the leaders of a large pork processing plant. We were looking for better ways to lead and better ways to reduce turnover.

I asked these leaders, "What do you do here?" One leader from the kill floor of the plant blurted out, "We kill hogs!" For the past several months I had worked with the leaders in every part of the plant and yes, he was right—we killed hogs. We processed over 15,000 a day in fact. I smiled and agreed with him. "But, why do we kill hogs?" I asked. After some silence came the answer, "To feed people." "Yes!" That is the motivation or the purpose of agriculture, "To feed people!"

I am not suggesting a mind game of any kind, but I am underscoring the need to focus on the real purpose of work. The need to reframe our work for the purpose of authentically motivating self and others. Every one in the world knows the value of good food. I can get motivated to do even the difficult aspects of a job if I better focus on the ultimate purpose. Those in agriculture help to feed the world! That is a noble and a valued enterprise!

In what ways am I making a real difference? Am I motivated about making a difference?

CHAPTER 8
DEPRESSION

Depression is the "common cold" of mental and emotional aliments. Some reports estimate that approximately nineteen million people suffer from depression each year. Other reports claim that as many as half of all Americans suffer from depression at some point in their life. Depression is likely to effect you or someone that you lead.

Depression is more that just feeling down, or blue, or discouraged. For the purposes of this chapter, depression is a feeling of hopelessness or gloom that lasts for more than one week and begins to effect our ability to lead and to cope with every day pressures of life. Some of the signs that depression is effecting you might be things like feelings of sadness or emptiness. Depression can also cause a lack of interest in things that normally you would have found some joy in.

Depression is like constantly viewing our world and all of our circumstances through a window that is dirty. If the window you view life through is filled with smudges and dirt and grime it makes everything appear discouraging and hopeless even though the facts are positive and should lead us to having more hope. As you try to encourage someone who is depressed you may say to them "look on the bright side," the problem is that these people looking through their "muddied window" stand in amazement that you can see anything bright about any situation. The problem with discouragement and depression is that the window they are looking through makes **everything** look bad.

It is especially important for a leader to find ways to combat depression quickly. Why? The leader's depression affects not only their own personal life and perspective on the job, it also affects every one else on their team and in their company. Some of the symptoms of depression involve having difficulty concentrating and making decisions. It is easy to see why this would be detrimental to a leader who needs to make decisions every day. Other things that characterize a depressed person are feelings of fatigue, agitation, restlessness, and irritability. Again, it is easy to see how these problems affect not only a leader but also everybody within their influence.

How do I quickly get out of the grasp of depression?

What is causing my depression?

Make a list of things that are bothering you and causing you anxiety.

Ask yourself if there is anyone you are angry at or any circumstances that are causing you anxiety.

Your answers will lead you to the next course of action. Take action on even small things you can control. For instance if you are angry with someone, either forgive them and go on, or confront them—sharing with them how you feel and how they have offended you. Continuing to take no action will probably continue the depression.

If it is a situation or life circumstance that is causing anxiety, the same action step is appropriate. What can I do to effectively begin to confront the situation that is bothering me? Some situations I cannot change or at least I cannot change right away. I can always change or at least examine my own attitude toward the situation. Can I change my mental position in regard to a certain situation that bothers me? Can I take action, even small steps, in making the circumstance more tolerable? What step can I take to solve the problem?

In recent studies at The University of Iowa, scientists have concluded that "take-charge conscientious people" are more likely to live longer. **In other words, you should think like Tiger Woods not like Woody Allen."**

Pessimism and depression can be deadly to your health. "In the study of one hundred and seventy four men and women who suffered from chronic kidney disease, the researchers found those who were prone to excessive worry and general anxiety were nearly forty percent more likely to die over a four year period than the average patient." Allen Christensen, a professor of psychology and internal medicine at the University of Iowa and lead author of the study (July 2002 issue of *Health Psychology*), concludes two major things: One, pessimism and discouragement among patients in the study caused them to not follow through with treatments that were prescribed to them, causing further health problems. Two, the study concludes that "patients that have chronic negative emotions tend to be immune suppressed." The bottom line seems to be the more we are depressed the easier it is to be depressed.

One of the common things that causes depression is loss of hope. Ask yourself how much hope you have that your company or your organization will be able to meet the challenges that you face today or the challenges that you will face tomorrow. A leader that has great hope concerning their own abilities and the abilities of their employees will approach the day much differently than those who have little hope that things will change or get better. What are some things you can do that will, even in small ways, improve your optimism and hope?

Am I physically or mentally worn out?

Depression has not only a psychological side to it, but also a physical one. It is quite logical that if I am fatigued it will bring on feelings of hopelessness or helplessness. Sometimes the best step you can take to relieve depression is to take a break.

How much change am I experiencing?

The deeper question might be: Am I experiencing too much change too fast? There is direct relationship between too much change and high levels of stress. We are all aware that we need to change and change quickly. This is all fine and good as long as it does not become excessive. Too much change can result in a feeling of being overwhelmed which can result in depression. One good technique to handle lots of change is to make two lists. Write down on one list all the things that are changing, and create a list right beside it with all the things that won't change. Try to think about the things that are positive and that are not changing in your life. You may have a stable and constant friend. Your faith in God may be steadfast. Your faithful dog will be there when you get home and Fido does not care whether you conquered the world today, or whether it conquered you—he just loves you. I like to look at the sunset or the sunrise and recognize that these events have been going on long before I arrived. They will continue right through this difficulty. Some things are good and they are constant and we can count on them.

The analogy of the sunset or the sunrise brings us to the next point and that is to make sure we view things from a long-term perspective.

Will the situation that is bothering me now really be that important long term?

When I was growing up, my dad would face difficult situations and say, "it won't matter in a hundred years." Some things that seem like a mountain to me today really won't make a lot of difference long term. Take the long term approach and focus your energies on things that do make a difference long term, and not on those things that are trivial.

Remind yourself of your mission and some clear meaningful goals!

Our current situation may, in reality, be that we are in the valley. But our goals can lead our thinking and our actions to the first steps that will take us again to the mountain top of great accomplishments and great hope. While we are in the valley it is key to anticipate what steps need to be taken that will lead us to victory.

Should I contact someone in my support system?

Everyone needs to cultivate his or her own support system. Many people naturally have a support system. It could be helpful to call a friend and just talk to them about the situation or ask them for their encouragement. My mom is a great encourager, and I have often benefitted from her spirit of support and encouragement.

It may be that you can turn to a hobby that you are always successful with and this will give you time to think through what is bothering you. Another part of the support system might be a pet that gives unconditional acceptance to you. Mortie is one of our family dogs. He is especially good at lots of unconditional acceptance. When I arrive home, he always seems glad to see me, he always stops whatever he is doing and bounds over to the car to greet me. He is never too busy for me. Mortie never asks me difficult questions. He never wonders why I am getting older. He never mentions the extra pounds I have put on. He never wonders if I have conquered the world or if it has conquered me. He just accepts me. Mortie just seems to clearly communicate encouragement as he nuzzles my leg or looks up at me. I have found one other thing that is very positive about Mortie. No matter what I tell him he never repeats it to anyone. He seems to understand my moods and seems to agree with nearly any position I take.

Having people in our lives that unconditionally accept us is a great bonus in overcoming depression. It is a great gift to have a friend or relative that cares about you and believes in you no matter what has happened this week. It is important to realize we can turn the tables and help someone else. Helping someone else is sometimes the best medicine to overcoming discouragement in our own lives.

To most of us depression can come on the heels of being a little too self-centered. Getting out and helping other people, seeing new sights, hearing new sounds that aren't always centered on me is an important part in gaining perspective. Sometimes it is important to get away even if its just in our minds for a few minutes.

It is important to realize that long-term depression is nothing to ignore. It may be important to get professional help from health providers that can give more insight to our physical and our mental well being. The good news is that depression is usually a highly treatable condition. The bad news is that depression left untreated can be a threshold to many other physical and emotional problems. This is especially true of people in leadership positions. Leaders that suffer from depression not only diminish their own effectiveness but can also end up short-circuiting the very life of their organization.

CHAPTER 9
FAILURE

The first question we need to grapple with is "How do we define failure?" I fully realize it is very popular to say there are no absolutes and that everything is relative. With that philosophy we can define any term anyway we'd like. After all "everything" is relative. However, I do not believe everything is relative, or that mankind holds a position of determining all truth. I like what noted author and speaker Zig Ziglar said in a devotional he delivered recently: "Many people say God said it, I believe it, that settles it! I'm here to tell you that if God said it it doesn't matter if I believe it or not, that settles it."

There are some realities all of us need to face in regard to failure. On one hand, yes we do fail. On the other hand, even with failure can come some success.

For instance, a number of years ago I decided to run for the House of Representatives in the state of Iowa. The overall objective was to win the house seat. As a part of accomplishing that objective we set a number of smaller but related goals. The first goal was to raise twice as much money as anyone ever had raised in that district before. We accomplished that goal. The second goal was to win over eight thousand votes (which in any previous election had always resulted in winning the seat). We accomplished that goal. I also set a goal to make many new friends and network with hundreds of people in pursuit of the House seat. I accomplished that goal in abundance. The long and the short of it is, we accomplished every goal that we had set and yet lost the election. Why? More people turned out to vote that year than in any year in the history of the district. Although we achieved our vote goal, we ended up losing the election by several percentage points. Of course, now the question is: Was the experience a failure or a success? In many ways it was a success and I look back at it with great memories. In another sense, it was a failure. With forty six percent of the vote, they don't let you go down and press the red and green buttons at the state house. We had lost the election—that is a reality. But it is also a reality that I had gained scores of friends and had many opportunities that continued for the next decade to shape my life and my business. So, in that sense it was very much a success.

Have you clearly defined success and failure?

For over a decade I have been a private pilot. One of the vital, unchangeable truths about flying is that it is important to have just as many landings as you have takeoffs! For me, the toughest thing about learning to fly was how to correctly use the radio and communicate with other pilots and the control tower. I have found the second most difficult thing to be landing. Obviously it is important to have good landings! The question is, "What is a successful landing?" As a pilot's experience and airport-time increase, he begins to pick up on certain truisms about flying. One of those truisms goes like this: "Any landing you can walk away from is a successful landing." Personally, at first I didn't like that definition. I preferred a more perfectionistic definition of a successful landing. One that has no bumps, no skips, no hops—just grease it in. You know, the landing where the transition from air to ground is seamless. With that definition, I am convinced that I have had only one successful landing. I remember it well, it was on an almost deserted grass landing strip at a very small airport next to a small town. The landing went perfectly. On touch down, my passenger turned to me and in some surprise asked, "Are we down?" I was almost as surprised! The landing was a stunning success—no bump, no skip, no hop, just a seamless transition from air to ground!

In the realities of life, whether it is flying or business or any organization, I think it is better to have a realistic definition of success and failure. I am glad to report that I have been able to walk away from every landing I have made. Therefore I consider them all successful.

I remember landing at an airport one time. After landing I taxied off the runway and turned around to look at the runway. I then saw another plane coming in. The problem was this plane did not have its wheels down. The plane was only fifteen feet above the concrete runway. Instinctively, I pushed the communication button on my yolk and skipped all the normal formality of identifying myself and who I was communicating with and simply yelled, "Your wheels aren't down, your wheels aren't down!" The warning came too late for the pilot to pull up, but he did manage to belly in on the relatively soft turf beside the runway, rather than the harsh concrete.

The scene seemed quite surreal, like something I should be seeing on a training film. The plane came to a shuddering halt and I held my breath waiting for flames. The flames did not come, and within a couple of seconds an elderly man popped out of the airplane and slowly surveyed the damage. Meanwhile, I was still trying to find a place to park my airplane as rescue workers descended on the runway. The pilot was the only one aboard the airplane and he survived the landing unscratched. I thought to myself as I finally shut my engine down—"Successful landing... he walked away!"

A number of years ago, I met a man with a strategy to make his life failure proof. What he meant by failure proof is simple: No matter what happened, he would always learn something! Whether he missed the mark, or didn't successfully complete a task, or whatever the result might be, he would always be a success because he would learn from it and apply what he learned to the next challenge in his life. There is much truth in his failure-proof approach to life. No matter what happens we can learn from it and therefore it has some gain.

Are you like leather or like stone?

Leaders need to think of themselves as being like leather, not like stone. What happens if I take a huge hammer and repeatedly strike a rock? The answer is, eventually the rock will start to splinter and crack and crumble. What if I take that same huge hammer and in the same manner strike a very thick piece of leather? The answer is, the leather will certainly show the marks of being hammered but will bounce back. The leather is more supple and will be able to regain its basic shape and survive hundreds and hundreds of blows from that hammer. Leaders need to be more like the thick piece of leather than some solid rock. We need the ability to bounce back from failure to learn from it and to apply that knowledge to the next circumstance. The question is—does failure cause us to crack up or can we learn from the blows of failure?

It is important to have a gyroscope that will cause us to right ourselves following upsets and times when we miss the mark. Courage to get back up and get back into life is crucial!

"There can be no failure for a man who has not lost his courage."

(Orison Sweet Minden)

How can I best analyze the situation and the cause of failure?

There are three basic questions that you might consider as you analyze the situation of failure.

1. What part did I have in this failed situation?
2. What part did others have in this failure?
3. What part did the the process have in causing this failure?

Let's start with the third question. There are some situations when even the best of leaders would find their result to be a failure. I remember talking to a highly respected leader who was probably one of the best in his field. He described a situation a colleague of his was facing and I remember him saying, "I don't know what to do in that situation, I'm sure I would have failed as well." I could hardly believe my ears. I thought there would be no situation this leader could not handle. The reality is, there are some situations where everyone would end up experiencing failure.

Let's consider the second question. There is no reason to scapegoat and blame others for things that we could change. But it is a reality that sometimes others are responsible for a large part of a failure. For instance, in a business relationship it takes two or more parties to create a successful team. But it only takes one of them to create a fraudulent and failed business. The same thing is true in relationships; it takes two willing partners to create a happy marriage, but only one unwilling partner to cause a failed marriage.

The first question refers to how much of the failure was something that I could control. Of course, we want to question what can be learned from that and how can we avoid those mistakes in the future. In this arena we have lots of extremes and lots of people in between. The first extreme, is that we might say we are to blame for nothing and it is never our fault, and it is the fault of some other circumstance. That extreme is probably not true. The other extreme is that everything is our fault. Likewise, this extreme is probably not true either. Some people act as though they control everything—even the weather. And if there is a rainy day, it is probably their fault. That is not true—the whole world does not rest on your shoulders. Everything that goes wrong—including the weather—is not your fault. It is also true that there is probably something you can do to improve the situation. It is okay to be less than perfect. You do not have to reach the goal the very first time you try. Success may be found upon the shoulders of lessons learned from repeated failures.

You don't have to be perfect to be excellent. Make sure your definition of success does not involve perfection. No one is perfect nor will we achieve perfection in this life. But we can be excellent. We can be first in class. We can be better than last year. All these would be measures of success, although not perfect success.

Early on, most leaders learn a fundamental lesson about leadership. That lesson is that we can't please everybody. I like what Herbert Bernard Swope says about success: "I can not give you a formula for success, but I can give you a formula for failure; try to please everybody."

Failure sometimes has terrific hidden rewards. By that I mean sometimes failure is cleverly disguised as opportunity. Anyone who observes the lives of successful people realizes that many successful people have had terrific failures at different points in their life. These failures—although very costly and certainly not pleasant—have often provided the platform from which great successes were launched. As leaders, we experience those times of failure and look for the opportunity to make the best of it. We find a way to turn it inside out and make it an astounding success.

One of the very difficult things to do in the face of failure is to be grateful for the experience. But we might ask ourselves during even some of the bitterest failing experiences—are we grateful for the lessons and for the insights that they may provide? Many times there is a huge decision to be made in the face of failure. Am I going to learn from it and be grateful, or am I going to be bitter? If I make the decision to be bitter and focus on "poor me," then it turns into a downward spiral of continuing defeat and failure. Or, if I can muster the courage to be grateful even from the bitterest experience it can sometime become the upward spiral toward more success and wisdom.

One of the final questions we need to ask ourselves is—is there anyone else that I can help based on what I have learned? Sometimes those lessons that I have learned can be passed on to my children, or my coworkers. In our organizations, we need to carefully record times of failure and lessons learned so that leader, crews, and teams that follow us can avoid those potholes and gain advantage for our organization as we seek to better serve our customers.

CHAPTER 10
DEBILITATION

In medicine we might talk about a debilitating disease. This would be a disease that causes the body to grow weaker and more feeble. In our work habits are we engaged in anything that is debilitating? These would be habits that cause us to have less ability and diminished energy to face the challenges of the day. As we think about debilitating habits we might immediately think about drugs or alcohol or other abusive habits. True enough, these will cause our body and mental powers to be reduced and to be weakened. But I would like to draw our attention to more common things that we may be engaged in that end up causing us to be tired, fatigued, and reduce our ability to meet the current challenges.

For several years I served as Dean of Student Services in a small college. One of the not so delightful challenges of any dean of student services is the enforcement of policies and rules. Most years, I would start off with a fairly standard speech to the incoming freshman concerning the rules of the institution. One of the side trails that I would take them down involved rules no one should break. Of course they were thinking about the various rules in the student handbook and parking policies etc. My point, though, was more fundamental. I tried to reinforce to them that although many of them were young and had good health, they were still not above the rules that guide our human existence. Some of you will think you are above the rules and don't need much sleep. But toward the middle of the semester when sleep deprivation begins to take its toll, you will not be able to keep up in class, you will not be able to concentrate, or make decisions regarding what is best for you and your schedule. Every human needs sleep—especially those who are extremely busy. Recently, I read an article that claimed that twenty years ago the average

American received 8 hours of sleep a night. Today that average has fallen to 6.8 hours per night. Most leaders are very goal focused and driven people, but none of us can live above the rules. All of us need sleep.

Are you practicing debilitating sleep habits?

Another rule of human existence that none of us can escape forever is the need for refreshment and good balance. This goes beyond the need for sleep, to a need for things like joy, relaxation, and a reprieve from the daily grind. All of us have probably thought, "Yes, everyone else needs those times of refreshment but not me—I can grind this out and be more effective. I don't need to stop and smell the roses."

We can concentrate and work long hours for several days in a row, but then extreme hours begin to catch up with us. None of us are above the rules. A few years ago I helped with research concerning how long workers could perform effectively and efficiently. The research found that workers could work twelve-hour shifts very effectively for about three days in a row before they needed a break. Workers that worked eight hours could work about five days without needing a break. Workers that worked four or less hours a day could work nearly every day without any break. You can see that when, as a leader, you start to put in sixteen hour days it doesn't take long before it becomes debilitating rather than being of any gain to you as an individual—or even to your organization.

To work our way out of long hours it is important to take a look at our goals and make them more short term and more realistic. Sometimes it is important to make a short-term goal; for example, make it through the afternoon. Then promise yourself that you will take a couple of hours in the evening just to refresh. Start by getting a good night's sleep so you can face the challenges of the rest of the week. Two good questions to consider are:

What is the vital thing I need to focus on?

What are some things I can ignore at least for a short while?

If you are constantly battling fatigue, you need to look at your own physical condition. Is the fatigue a result of just simply being out of shape or is it something deeper? Are you overweight? Are you eating too much? Are you not eating enough? What causes your lack of energy to be a chronic problem? In your lifetime you are issued only one body. Whatever its characteristics, it is the only body you have and you had better develop habits that enable your body to function well for the rest of your life.

We have all heard the story about the old man and the young man chopping down trees in the forest. The old man would stop every so often and take the time to sharpen his ax. The young man eager to get more done would not stop but continued to whack away at tree after tree. In the middle of the afternoon, the young man was fatigued, completely out of energy, and was beginning to get less trees chopped than the older gentleman. Although the young man spent more time whacking away at trees, he actually achieved less than the old man who wisely stopped every so often to rest and sharpen his ax. The lesson, of course, is good for us at any age. It is not only a nice idea, but it is absolutely vital if we are to be effective in the long run. Stop and refresh yourselves often! The race you are in is more like a marathon than a sprint.

What can I do this week to develop habits that will refresh and recharge me so I can improve my abilities rather than reduce them?

If your energy levels are constantly low even though you are in good health, maybe the problem is that you are doing something that really doesn't naturally energize you. Maybe you are engaged in too many activities that you have no interest in or that do not naturally inspire and increase your energy levels. It may be a good time to ask:

Am I engaged in something that I can get excited about?

The final thing to look at is, are you actually trying to do too much? A number of years ago, an associate of mine seemed to enjoy pointing out how messy my desk was and how I didn't always keep up on my filing. Years later, as my associate took over some of the same responsibilities. I noticed that her desk also began to look pretty messy and she to didn't always get her filing done.

Without trying to seem like I was saying, "I told you so," I asked her about the messy desk and the problem with getting everything filed. Her response was very similar to mine when I was handling those jobs. There just isn't time to get everything done! While it was nice to know it wasn't just me, it was also an indication that some jobs are too much for any one person.

What responsibilities can I hand off to others?

Make three lists! The first list will contain those things that you want to **keep** and logically should keep as pertinent to your responsibilities. The second list will be of things you might be able to **share**. You will be able to give away forty percent of a responsibility, and keep sixty percent of the responsibility, and save some time and energy. The third list is the most fun to construct and is anything that you could just flat out **give away** to someone else. This, at first, may seem like an impossibility. But you might be surprised how people on your crew or in your organization would be pleased to take over some small tasks and relieve you of bits of responsibility. If you could get rid of one hour per week, that would begin to give you some breathing room to become more effective at the core requirements of your job.

Chapter 11
Managing Stress

The first thing to recognize is that there is a difference between good stress and harmful stress. As human beings we are well equipped to handle a great deal of stress. The problem comes when that stress becomes too much or we endure that stress for too long. Another important factor to consider is that different kinds of stress affect us all in different ways.

Everyone's strengths and abilities are different. The differences cause us to be stressed by different things. Although I would find it somewhat stressful to speak in front of a roomful of people for an hour, I would find that stress positive and a healthy challenge. But, place me in an accounting office and force me to make my living by entering data hour after hour, and you would probably find me swinging from the ceiling by noon. I would find the demands of that task very stressful, and soon it would begin to take its toll on me and probably those around me.

Good stress is what an athlete experiences before a big game, or an Olympian faces before the big race. Certainly we could agree that any sprinter would be under stress before the start of the race. However, the athlete can use the stress to produce world record times. In this scenario, the stress, although heavy, works in our favor to produce records that no one else has ever matched in the entire world. We can use this same principal at work. Good stress challenges us to perform at a level we have never been able to perform at before.

The key to keep in mind is that the Olympics take place only once every four years. Obviously we are expected to show up at work more often. Only the mediocre do their best every day. There will be times of great productivity and times when we are not so great in the everyday work schedule. The thing to remember is that we can handle lots of positive stress, if it is for a good cause and it plays to our strengths.

We might liken good stress to how we tune a stringed instrument. The strings on the violin must have just the right tension to play great music. Too much tension and they will break; too little tension, and they will not produce the notes needed to perform even a simple piece of music. The violin string will perform for a long time if it is used properly and kept in the right balance. It is important to put our team members and ourselves in the appropriate positions. If we take that violin string and try to pull a truck out of the ditch with it, obviously it will break. It was never intended for that kind of use. However, a heavy log chain might be under relatively little stress in performing the same task. It was made to pull heavy objects. However, it would probably perform poorly in an orchestra.

What types of bad stress am I experiencing?

Make a list of those things that you are experiencing that are causing you stress. According to the Annals of Occupational Hygiene, Vol. 33, the following are the ten most common job-related stress factors:
1. Not being organized or able to manage time effectively.
2. Having conflicts with workers or colleagues.
3. Feeling overwhelmed with the job.
4. Feeling unqualified to do the job.
5. Having too much or too little responsibility.
6. Not being able to meet dead lines.
7. Not being able to adapt to changes in the work routine.
8. Not being able to utilize skills and abilities.
9. Feeling that work is boring or meaningless.
10. Not getting any support from supervisors or managers.

Outside the job, things like money problems or relationship problems or health problems may be some top stressors in your life. Once you have completed a list of things that are stressing you, try to prioritize that list and choose the top two or three things that are causing you the most negative stress. Using those top items as your focus what are some things you can do to start managing the stress in a more productive way?

What can I do short term to begin to manage this negative stress?

Are there any processes we can improve?

Is there anything you can change about the way you go about doing work? Is there any process that you can improve? For instance, if paperwork is driving everybody nuts in the office area, get a small team together and think of ways to cut down on the paper work. If there is a copy machine that causes more stress than its worth maybe it would be good to get rid of it and purchase a new one or get it fixed once and for all. If schedules are constantly causing friction and stress, put together a small team and think of ways to improve the schedule.

Is there anything we can improve by way of communication?

When employees are not informed, they tend to make up answers to their questions. The answer created is often more fear-inducing or more stressful than the truth. It is proven again and again that even in difficult situations the organization that has good communication will have decreased stress levels. Even if the news is not good news, it is better to know it and be honest with one another than to wrestle with the fears that gossip and exaggeration will create.

Can we improve the trust level and the cohesion of our work group?

The least stressful work environments nurture a sense of closeness and cohesion with the team. The goal is to create an environment where people trust one another while they pursue the same goals. Your team needs to be focused on an objective that will best serve the purposes of the organization. A well-focused team will be able to ignore differences in order to reach the overall focus.

Some of the most stressful job situations occur when team members can no longer trust one another. Is there more energy and stress devoted to protecting our turf than there is to obtaining any given goal? Are we more worried about being tackled by other teammates than being challenged by our customers? A negative environment needs to be identified and changed by everyone; a new code of conduct should be developed that will nurture trust and appreciation.

How open am I to change?

Being open to change and to solutions that may break with some of the past paradigms is key to developing better solutions and to reducing stress. If I continue to have very little flexibility, I will probably continue to have a great deal of stress as the environment around me changes rapidly. Again, it is important to see ourselves as being supple like a thick piece of leather and not hard and inflexible like a rock.

Managing Stress Outside the Job

Outside the job, it is important to begin to develop a support system. These methods would be longer-term ways of dealing with stress. One important element of the support system is to have more than one source of encouragement or support that will enable us to better handle those inevitable days when stress overwhelms us. Everyone will experience situations in life that require a support system.

Few people would be so bold as to say that major negative events in their life don't cause them to be stressed and overwhelmed. Stresses like the loss of a spouse, a child running away, loss of your own health, or major financial problems will cause anyone to be deeply stressed. When these things happen in our lives, what do we do? When these events, or others like them, occur it is vital to have a support system. A support system is just like it sounds—it is someone or something you can lean on during especially stressful days. It is like having a large chair to support you rather than a one-legged stool.

One leg of the support system could be to have some kind of source of *unconditional acceptance*. These are people, or perhaps pets, that are part of our life and will accept us no matter what happens. It is important to cultivate the kind of friendship with someone where they will stick with you through thick and through thin. Some people find that their pet might be a source of unconditional acceptance. As I illustrated earlier in the book, our family dog Mortie can serve as a great source of unconditional acceptance.

A second leg of the chair that might support us during difficult days is some source of *unconditional love*. This would be somebody like maybe a favorite grandma that loves you no matter what happens in your life. You might have lost your job, or you might have been accused of a crime, but grandma still loves you.

Granted, she may not appreciate the fact that you lost your job, but none the less she demonstrates sincere and honest love for you. You are her grandchild no matter what you do.

Another leg of the chair might be *a good hobby*. Hobbies that do not add stress can be a great part of our support system. This kind of hobby is one that gives us satisfaction and some sense of accomplishment even when nothing else is providing that for us. A friend of mine was going through an unavoidable bankruptcy, and of course this caused a great deal of stress in his life. He found, during the darkest days of financial stress, that reading good novels was a really important part of his support system. Hobbies that involve healthy excercise are extremely important and give us healthy outlets in which to relieve stress.

My own experience and some research results back the idea that "People of faith" have a better support system than people of no faith. This fourth leg of the chair might give us a bigger picture; people of *faith* tend have a bigger picture of life. As we go through a very difficult time we might have the perspective that this will pass and God will help us to find better times ahead. This reasoning helps reduce the stress of the current problems. Also of course faith in a loving God can be a source of unconditional acceptance or unconditional love.

Obviously there are other parts of a support system that may be helpful for you. Whatever type of support system you nurture in your own life, make sure it has more than one point of support and make sure you are not too proud to use your support system. Life is a little like a car race, and if you think everything is under control you either don't understand the gravity of the situation or you are not driving fast enough.

How can I recognize stress among my team members?

If you see employees with a significant change in their behavior they might be experiencing the ravages of too much stress. Sometimes, increased absenteeism is a symptom of too much stress in the work place. Anger is another big indicator of stress. Everyone will probably become irritated or angry at some point, but when it becomes chronic, it may be caused by too much stress in the culture at our job.

"Those employees who experience the most stress are those who are in high demand/low control jobs" (*Working Smarter*, Nov. 1992)

There is probably no doubt in anyone's mind that the workplace is filled with more stress today than it was twenty or thirty years ago. One of the strategies that seems to help is to give the employees more say in what they do, and when it is scheduled. This is not always possible. If employees sense more control over the great demands put upon them, they will feel less stressed. This does not mean we can short circuit service to our customers, or shirk the duties that are pressed upon us. But it does mean we can talk about how to give employees more latitude when possible.

Many people start off their work career in manual jobs. Because they are good leaders, we promote them, and the nature of their work changes. The following observation is an important one to take note of: **"When the work is more mental than manual, the injuries will be too."** (source: Office Biology, Weiner and Brown, 1993)

As we end this chapter, here are six coping skills I have found helpful in dealing with stress:
1. Choose to look at the situation differently.
2. Don't take on a victim mentality rather take ownership of your life.
3. Practice preventive maintenance; be wise about your diet, exercise, rest, and relaxation habits.
4. Keep your goals and expectations realistic.
5. Share your feelings and seek support often.
6. Don't beat yourself up; monitor your self-talk and make sure it's mostly positive.

Chapter 12
Leading Through Change

Change means to alter, from one form to another. One of the basic questions we should ask ourselves is "Why should we change?" The answer is that if we don't change we might go out of business. Perhaps the best reason to change is because our customers have changed. When our employees ask the question, "Why should we change?" Often they are really asking, "What's in it for me to make this change?" This question is a valid and logical one.

Many times as I work with teams and other groups I ask them the question, "Do most people like to change?" The response that these groups give me is almost a unanimous, "No people do not like to change." The next question I ask is, "Do you like to change?" The answer to this question is much more divided. But the majority ends up saying, "Yes I like to change."

If people ask me, "Do I like to change?" my response is, "That all depends." If someone wants to change my yearly income by doubling it, I'm all for that change. Why? Because it is a positive change and I can see clearly what's in it for me or for other people I care about. On the other hand if someone wants to take away my income and replace it with some complex and difficult to understand formula, that may or may not benefit me, I am probably going to be against that change.

I don't believe people are against change. I believe they are against change that they have no say about and in which they do not see some clear advantage. This does not mean that all people are always just looking out for themselves. What it does mean is that people are naturally suspicious of change that will not clearly help the organization or help their situation. People do not like to have change thrust upon them. They are much more likely to be in favor of change if they have some meaningful input.

There are many things in the workplace, as well as our own lives, that we have little control over. We do however have a great deal of control over how we respond to those changes.

How will we respond to the forces that drive change?

Analyze the following list of eight things that propel change in our workplace. Which of the eight will affect you the most? How will they begin to affect you in the months and years ahead? How should we respond to these changes?

Forces that are Propelling Change

1. Continuous quality improvement.
2. Technology advancements.
3. Terrorism and security concerns.
4. Customer service.
5. A constant call for more convenience and speed.
6. Age and generation waves.
7. Life values and life styles.
8. Mass customization.

Most of these forces speak for themselves. The question we need to ask is, "How will they effect our organization?" The first force demands that we ask the question, "What changes in our processes and systems can we make to produce higher quality products and services?" The second force is obviously the advancing technology; how will technology change our business in the next eighteen months? The third one has to do with heightened awareness that we all have of the threat of terrorism. It has changed the landscape of many organizations. What changes in security and identification of personnel may be needed in our organization immediately? The fourth one has to do with customer service. It seems that some organizations still have a great deal of changes that are needed in order to better serve customers. Some organizations still believe they are doing the customer a favor by paying any sort of attention to them. More and more decisions are being made by the customer based simply on their perception of good customer service. The fifth one has to do with the combination of faster speed and, at the same time, more convenience. How easy is it to do business with your organization? How fast can you take care of customer's needs? The sixth one has to do with the age waves or generations that are making their way through our population. For instance, the baby boom generation has been famous for how it has changed nearly every institution that it has passed through. How will the baby boom generation change your organization? How will the generation X-ers change your organization? The seventh one has to do with the changing values and life styles throughout our culture. For example, a great number of people are beginning to value free time or time off more than more money. How will this lifestyle change affect your organization? The eighth force is mass customization. Everyone wants to have it his or her way. Everyone wants the advantages of the assembly line, but still want to have the uniqueness of having a one-of-a-kind. How will this desire affect your organization?

It is very important that people throughout your organization understand that as a leader you are not laying awake nights trying to figure out how to make their lives miserable by changing all sorts of things in the work environment. These eight propellants of change largely drive the need for change. It is not any one person's fault, it is not your fault, it is just a fact of how things around us are changing. We do not have to respond to the changes, but what will the consequences be if we do not?

I often hear the statement, "The only constant is change." Frankly, I do not believe this is true. One of the difficulties of managing change is the realization that some things do not change. And actually, **some things should not change.** Think about the following list of things that organizations purposely try not to change. See if any of them should be maintained at your organization.

1. High trust levels.
2. A focus on customers and serving others.
3. The team work values of a shared vision, shared values, and shared beliefs.
4. Personal time devoted to developing people.
5. Maintaining an action focus.
6. Working hard.
7. The need for mutual respect in the organization.
8. The opportunity to have a sense of significance and fulfillment in our organization.

It is a good strategy to point out to people a list of things that need to change, and a list of things that will never change in our organization. The stability of some things that have lasting value and lasting importance will help all of us to take on the challenges of those things that need to change. Change is not so bad if I can clearly see the reason for it, and if I can be a part of helping to shape that change.

The following ten principles of change I have shared with many companies. Hopefully you will find some of them to be helpful as you face the difficulties of change.

1. Anticipate Change.

As leaders you need to be thinking about where the organization or the team needs to be in the next year, or in the next two years. Start to anticipate what kind of training needs, material needs, machinery needs will present themselves and prepare for those changes.

2. Plan out the Change.

It is important to clearly plan out the stages of any major change. Sometimes a Gantt chart or some kind of flow chart will help people visualize how the steps of the change all fit together, and how they will all be networked when they are completed.

3. Use teams in the change process.

For some parts of the change process, establishing a team to help figure out the details is good strategy. This promotes ownership of the change and gives us more ideas to better execute any given change.

4. Really communicate and listen.

Every leader tries to communicate and most try to listen. But it is especially important during times of rapid change. Communicate again and again the reasons for change, the procedures involved, and some of the benefits of change. We then need to listen to some of the concerns and worries of people within our organization. Sometimes we can provide ready answers to those concerns. It is important to listen and to communicate again and again, in many different ways, what we are trying to accomplish.

5. Paint the picture of outcomes.

Most changes have a painful side to them. It is important, however, to have people picture the pleasant (or at least the positive) outcomes of change— not just the pain of getting there. For instance, I am trying to lose some weight, so I don't want to just picture myself in agony on the treadmill; instead, I want to picture myself forty pounds lighter and enjoying the freedom of better health and new clothes.

6. Create support networks.

If the change is truly huge, you may want to establish a network of people who can support one another. If suddenly my health has a huge change and I discover I have cancer, we can all see the advantage of having a network of people who have gone through the same challenge and had victory. It is encouraging and the sharing of ideas is vital to handling large doses of change.

7. Follow through on details.

Details are especially important during change. During changes all of us have more questions and more concerns and it is important to have great follow through on the details that will deal with those questions.

8. Prepare for the price of change—mistakes.

Hopefully we aren't so foolish as to promise that if we make this change everything will be perfect. Actually, we need to prepare people for the reality that in making the change we will also make some mistakes. But we will learn from them and, in the end, things will be better.

9. Keep steps of change simple.

It is important to keep the steps of change simple. It is much easier to tackle a stairway where steps are six inches tall rather than eighteen inches tall.

10. Lead by example-demonstrate how you are changing.

If our team sees us making dramatic changes and learning from some of our mistakes, they will be more likely to make the changes demanded of them.

Any large change demands much of us and of our people. There are real fears and real concerns as we face some of the huge challenges of change. I like what Eddie Rickenbacher says: **"Courage is doing what you are afraid to do. There can be no courage unless you're scared."**

CHAPTER 13
COMMUNICATION

As I work with many different organizations, it is clear that communication is usually one of the top three challenges for every organization. Many people underestimate how difficult it is to clearly communicate. Frankly, communication is just plain hard work!

Each of us is bombarded with thousands of messages pleading with us for our attention each day. It is no wonder that people become numb to nearly every form of communication. Just to survive, we have to ignore some things that are vying for our attention. Of course, it can be a major problem if we begin to ignore crucial messages that are given in the workplace.

Another huge problem is the fact that even though I think I am communicating clearly, the receiver is interpreting my words in a different way than I intended. If I am trying to listen, I still have the problem of people starting from different assumptions, having different definitions of the same words, and reading into my communication things that were never intended. All of these factors are a challenge to communication before we even consider language barriers that are a part of many work situations.

The communication equation contains two major parts. There is the sending part and the receiving part. First, let's consider the receiving part of communication. It is interesting that in our colleges and universities nearly every one of them has some kind of speech major but none of them, to my knowledge, have a listening major. We probably all need to do more study and more training in the area of effective listening. After all, probably two thirds of our communication time is spent listening.

As we think of the communication process or the sending part of the equation, consider the fact that there are three major parts of communication:

1. The words we use.
2. Our tone of voice.
3. Our body language or expressions.

If we were to make a pie diagram of these three, what percentage of the communication load would the words carry, what percentage would the tone of voice carry, and what percentage would the body language carry? It is surprising to many people that the words carry only about ten percent of the load of communication, the tons of voice forty percent, and body language fifty percent or more.

Just to test out these percentage, think about the situation where someone is telling you one thing with their words and yet you pick up an entirely different message from their tone of voice. Do you believe what they are saying with their words, or what they are saying with their tone of voice? Most people agree they believe the tone of voice. The same thing can be said of body language.

It is hard to believe that someone is excited about my work performance if their tone of voice and their body language doesn't agree with their words. The receiver is likely to conclude that your motives are to butter them up so that you can ask them to work overtime in the next sentence.

Think about the fact that babies only a few days old can interpret and understand tone of voice and body language, but it will take them a couple more years to begin to master any words. Even across language groups, people pick up on your tone of voice and your body language. This is probably a great advantage where there are multiple languages spoken and multiple cultures in the workplace.

The key to great communication is to be sure that you align all three of these pieces of the communication pie. Make sure your word, your tone of voice, and your body language are all saying the same things. If we do this, then communication will be much clearer.

How is the alignment of my words, my tone of voice, and my body language?

Let's go back to the listening side of the communication equation. The fact is that different people listen with different perspectives. We all value different things in any communication package. There are at least five key things that people listen for in any message. The problem is that each of us values one or more of these five differently.

What do you listen for the most in any communication package?

What does your audience listen for in any communication package?

What do you listen for the most in any communication?
1. The facts

>Facts, data, or content is what some people listen for the most; they don't care about how someone delivers it, or if it's filled with nice stories, they are just looking for the facts.

2. Logic

>Some people look for and most appreciate the reasoning behind the speaker's arguments. If the sender doesn't have good logic these listeners will start to tune them out.

3. Emotion

>Some people listen for a speaker's emotion or sincerity. If the speaker isn't sincere, then they begin to ignore the message even if it may be filled with great facts and great logic.

4. Motive

>Some listeners are tuned into what the true motive of the speaker is. Is their motive pure and trustworthy or do they sense the speaker is really trying to trick them? If the speaker is trying to deceive them, this listener will tune out immediately.

5. Enjoyment

>Some listener's first and foremost look for a speaker's wit and whether or not they will enjoy the message. Do they have a sense of humor and will they tell some enjoyable stories to underscore their points? If the message doesn't have some enjoyment to it then why should we listen?

The key purpose for analyzing how we like to listen and how our audience likes to listen is to apply the golden rule of listening. Speak to them using the style they best listen to or how they enjoy receiving the message. We have to consider how they will best listen to our message.

If we are going to present the annual budget to owners or to the president and his cabinet, we probably need to emphasize the facts and the data involved in our message. Other important parts would probably be logic, reasoning, and they will also be listening for our motive. Too many jokes and this group will wonder what we are up to.

Another great question to consider as we analyze our audience is:

What will most effectively influence my audience to listen and accept my message?

Again, you might consider the five perspectives listed above and which ones will most influence your particular audience.

One of the most important things to do early in the conversation or the message is to identify why the listener should continue to listen. Everyone is tuned into the fictional radio station entitled WIIFM.

What's In It For Me?

Everyone is tuned into this station and if we can address that early within the first sentence or two they probably will continue to listen.

If we are attempting to give a safety talk, it is important to answer the question of what's in it for them at the beginning of the talk. We might show some graphic pictures of accidents or tell a true story of someone who was recently injured. That begins to get across the message of what's in it for them. They can avoid the hospital and lots of pain—that's what's in it for them.

A second important thing that almost everybody listens for, are any kind of messages that help them feel more significant or important. This does not mean that people are selfish, it is just a basic human need to find some kind of fulfillment and significance in life. If your message has something to do with why they are significant people will listen.

One of the exercises I often do with teams is what I call a strength building exercise. What this means is that everybody sits in a small circle of maybe five or six people and one by one go around focusing on one individual in the circle telling one thing they see about them that is a strength. No one ever falls asleep during this exercise! People listen intently as each colleague points out one strength that they see in them.

How can I picture my message?

Think of how you can picture your message. How can you tell a story that captures the essence of your message? Or how can you show a picture on the overhead that communicates the essence of your message? The fact of the matter is that we all think in pictures. The more clear pictures that fill your message the better chance that your message will be received clearly.

CHAPTER 14
ASKING QUESTIONS

Often, good clear questions are more powerful than good clear admonishment. Why? If I tell someone what to think, they are still not thinking. However, a good clear question almost forces us to begin to think for ourselves. Personal thinking will result in personal decisions of commitment. Personal, heartfelt commitment of people in our organizations will accomplish more than telling our employees they should be committed.

It is both important to ask yourself questions and to ask your organization good questions. For many years, I have believed the foundation for good questions to be centered in six simple words. I call these the six servants of planning. The six words are:

What? Why? How? Who? When? Where?

The first question is "What?" What are we going to do? What is our mission?

Why are we doing this? What is the ultimate purpose behind it and why?

How are we going to go about accomplishing what we want to accomplish? How will we execute the details in the plan?

Who will help us? Who will be on our team? Who do I need to compliment my strengths?

When will we do the different parts of the plan? When will it be finished? When will we start?

Where will this all take place? Where do we need to position ourselves?

I use each of these six servants of planning whenever I plan training for a company. I can think through each of the six on the phone as I talk to a potential client. I use each of the six as I count down through them to plan out most any important venture. I use each of them to plan out things for my own life.

If you put together a plan and begin to execute that plan and still something is going wrong, you might ask yourself at least one more question. That question is, "What is still missing?" Or, "What do I still not see?" If our plan is not working it is important not to keep repeating it. Anyone who repeats again and again the same thing expecting different results is dabbling in a mild form of insanity. If what you are doing is not working, ask yourself what is still missing.

One of the important things that any leader should be constantly engaged in, is asking for good wisdom from others. Many times I have found what I need to make something work by simply reflecting upon it with a friend. A friend can ask me good questions or immediately point out things that they see that are deficient in my plan. Ask for good advice.

The ability to ask yourself good questions and to ask others is a lifetime pursuit. However, in the following list you will find a few questions that I believe will get you started toward productive and useful questions:

1 How would I tell a ten-year-old child what the purpose of our department is?
2. What is our ultimate purpose?
3. What are our strengths and our resources?
4. What is our ultimate mission?
5. What is our plan?
6. Who can I find to help me?
7. Who can I network with outside of our organization that can help?
8. Where will the adversity come from?
9. What will be some of the problems in accomplishing our objectives?
10. When will we begin?
11. How will I measure progress?
12. How will we measure success?
13. Why am I doing what I am doing?
14. Where will all of this lead us in two years, five years, and ten years?
15. If this idea fails what will we do?
16. If this idea produces ten times what we think it will what will we do?
17. What other member of my organization can I call?
18. What other sources could aid me?

A final thought about questions. Obviously questions are an important part of good leadership. However, there is a dark side to some questions. Some questions don't produce clear answers. Some questions I can't answer. Some questions can actually make things cloudier and more uncertain. Although questions are an important part of leadership, they are not to be treated as some new toy we play with for no good reason.

No one doubts that in everyone's life there are things for which we don't have a great answer. For instance haven't you ever wondered why kamikaze pilots wore helmets? There are many things we do know. That clear knowledge demands our clear action.

There are some life questions that have no clear answers; but, I find plenty to concern myself with as a result of those questions for which do have clear answers!

CHAPTER 15
DECISION MAKING

One of the most difficult tasks for a leader is that of making a decision. One of the reasons for this difficulty is often that the decision needs to be made around some sort of problem. Often we are deciding how to resolve a problem. Everyone else can make the easy decisions but it's up to the leader to make those decisions that revolve around problems.

Perhaps all of us have found ourselves in the quagmire of decision making where by we make one decision to solve one problem and we actually create two more problems. This happens because problem solving is like the tip of an iceberg. There are many more things to be considered when making sound decisions. If we do not make sound decisions then we will only be making more icebergs.

Instead of problem solving, it is important to fix processes within our systems. If I can fix the fundamental process that causes the problem many times the problem will not reoccur.

1. Define the current process.

In this step, describe the process that is giving you the problem. I have found that flow charting the current process is often a great way of clearly defining what is going on. Also during this process, begin to collect all sorts of data. What are needed are facts and figures and collective perceptions of people inside and outside the process. My teams have often found that some problems aren't nearly as large as they perceived them to be and some problems are much larger than we thought they were. The only way to determine this is by good, solid data.

2. Analyze the current process.

The purpose of this step is to gain knowledge about the day-to-day, week-to-week performance that we are trying to fix. What are the trends, or the patterns, of the performance of the problem process? In this stage, it's important to find out what the biggest parts of the problem are. Work on those first, because we do not have time to work on everything.

3. Analyze the causes for current outcomes.

In this step we want to look for the root cause that is behind the problems in the process. We all know that it will do no good to fix the symptoms of the problem. We must peel away the outer layers to get to the root causes and fix the problem at the cause level. For example one golf course created a team to improve the process of their weekly staff meetings. As they collected data they found that one of the biggest complaints about the meetings is that they were too long. It did not take much effort to time how long each meeting lasted. The next objective was to ask the question "Why?" Why do the staff meetings last so long? As the team continued to collect data, we found that some of the reasons for long meetings were not having a clear agenda, people arguing, going down "bunny trails" until everyone was exhausted, not starting on time, and not coming to the meeting prepared. The team suggested a format for determining the agenda one week ahead of time. The team also came to consensus on rules of conduct during the meeting. Team leaders were required to be prepared and make sure others were prepared to discuss points on the agenda. Rules were enforced. If you were not prepared, they skipped that part of the agenda and it went on next week's agenda. A meeting facilitator was trained and led the meetings. A clear way of making decisions was determined by the team. Each meeting started on time and those who were late were assessed a small fine. As the team continued to measure the lengths of the meetings the chart on the wall constantly went down in the number of hours and minutes that the meetings lasted. The team was beginning to see lots of success. Obviously shortening the meeting time was not the only objective; another objective was to have the meetings be more effective and helpful to the staff. Those objectives were also beginning to see results. The key thing was to attack the problem of long and fruitless meetings at the roots of what caused that problem. If we fix the causes the results likewise would get better.

4. Develop the improvement ideas and the implementation plan.

As the root causes are uncovered, it is important to develop an improvement plan and how we are going to implement that plan in our organization. It is important that those who are working on the improvement idea are also the shepherds of the implementation of those ideas. If you set the teams up so that they report to you, and you're responsible for implementation it will often cause trouble. The trouble is, if someone else has to implement this, then I become a lot more creative in what I think they should do. If I have to implement it, then I'm much more reasonable and much more pragmatic about what will work and what will not.

5. Implement the improvement ideas and study the results.

It is important of course to implement the ideas for improvement but equally important is the follow-through of studying the result of that implementation. Often we do not know how well the ideas have worked or if they have worked at all. The discipline of studying the report will also derail any naysayers as to whether or not the process improvement was successful.

6. Engraft the improvements into your organization.

Many good ideas have been implemented only to find months later, as the team turns its back on the implementation, people go back to the old way of doing things. That's why it is essential to make the improvements the way we do business now. We must engraft them into our organization so that they will weather the storms of implementation just like any other well-supported process.

7. Plan for more continuous improvement of processes.

Step number seven takes us full circle as we begin to anticipate where our next challenges will come from. What problems do we need to work on next before they become a crisis? A good source of ideas about what to work on next comes from our customers. Another group to constantly ask for ideas is the front line workers. They often can sense problems even before leadership clearly sees them.

Teams improving processes is only one way of making better decisions. The leader will need to make a good number of decisions on their own without the aid of a team. It is still important to gather lots of facts, figures, and data in order to make those decisions. It is still important to attack problems at their roots. It is almost more important to do follow-through study to prove that your decisions were sound and have resulted in a good impact on your organization. Gathering data on how your ideas have saved the organization money or solved deficiencies will help fend off naysayers in the future.

Chapter 16
Budget Leadership

Who among us truly understands money? I fear that those who claim they do are the most dangerous. Those who claim not to know how to handle money have in their ranks a few that actually do know how to best use money. It is important that at least someone understands money within any organization. But all of us need to understand one important fact about budgets and money and that is this: money is a tool.

Money is as much a tool as any computer, tractor, or saw. Budgets and money are vehicles that we use to accomplish many of the tasks in our organizations.

One of the ironies of money is that there is a large disconnection between having money and being successful or happy. Many organizations have more than adequate money but are not successful. Other organizations have very little money but become very successful. There seems to be no direct correlation. Certainly on a personal level, we all have observed many people who have very little money, poor health, and other terrific obstacles, and yet they are very happy and satisfied in life. On the other hand, many people who have money, great health, and few obstacles are unhappy, confused, and frustrated with life.

"Happiness is not based on money. And the best proof of that is our family" (Christina Onassis)

It is important to have a balanced and intelligent view of the part that money plays in our organization and in our own personal lives. I like what one of my sisters says concerning money: "Money isn't important unless you don't have any." It is easy to be cavalier about the need for money when you have plenty of it, but when budgets are extremely tight, or we are staring bankruptcy in the face, money becomes pretty important. But money is not all-important and should be viewed as a tool that we use in our organizations and in our personal lives.

"In regard to money: I don't necessarily like it, but it quiets my nerves." (Joe Lewis, *Quote Unquote*)

Is the process of establishing a budget and gaining approval clearly outlined in your organization? Is the process altered due to unexpected emergencies? I have worked with many colleges and municipalities that have a budget-making process that is similar to the swamp of the Everglades; they can't see the sea for all the sawgrass! It's very unclear how priorities are determined and how to establish any given budget when you're up to your armpits in alligators!

You can use a flow chart to clearly delineate the steps and the timeline for establishing your budget. Much confusion can be avoided if we simply push the timeline forward into the year so that we have time to think about the issues and the priorities that will drive next year's budget.

Do I know the process for establishing my budget?

Find someone within the organization that understands the budget-making process and finances to coach you in the first year or two of establishing your budget. It is one thing to understand the numbers in a given budget, it is quite another to understand how priorities are reached, what the real values are of the organization, and how one goes about investing new money in important programs and people.

Is there any way I can create win win collaborations with organizations outside of my own?

Many organizations face the same budget problems. It is important, therefore, to look outside our wall and see if there are any collaborative efforts that we could initiate with other organizations that would truly be a win-win situation. One example of this is in my own hometown. For years our community of about twenty five thousand residents wrestled with the desire to have an indoor swimming facility, racquetball courts, a public gymnasium, and weight room facilities. The advantages would be many for our community. The central problems were almost always the same, year after year. The community could figure out how to run the facility on a break-even basis, but could not afford the cost of the structure. The school could probably pass a bond issue that would allow the structure to be built, but could not afford to operate the facility. A collaborative solution was finally put together. The school would fund the project through a bond issue that passed overwhelmingly; the YMCA would administrate the facility and operate it on a day to day basis. The facility was connected directly to the high school and both the high school and the YMCA shared the parking lot. Part of this collaborative effort actually grew out of a smaller one that had been at work for several years. During some of the budget crunches of the early 1980s, a collaborative effort was initiated between the city, the county, and the school district. Each one of these organizations had some things in common like the need to mow lawns, remove snow, and to acquire dump trucks and earth moving equipment. It became apparent that if everyone had a full fleet of trucks for moving dirt, a full fleet of snow removal equipment, and a full fleet of mowers to mow lawns, all three groups would feel the economic pinch in a hurry. If, however, they could collaborate and share equipment through some kind of mutual agreement everyone could save money and we could have even better equipment. That kind of collaboration is exactly what took place.

There will be naysayers to any kind of collaborative idea, but try to work through some of the problems and you might be surprised at how much can be gained by way of relationships and monies saved. Think of a budget as money you are going to invest, not money that you are going to spend. In asking for larger budgets, how can you prove to a board or owner that you are going to invest this money and have some kind of tangible return on investment? If we are just going to spend it, it is understandable that people are reluctant to give us more money. If, however, we can demonstrate with data and good statistics that an investment of say five thousand dollars will save us eight thousand dollars over the next year, then leadership will be likely to fund that kind of budget investment. Pretend that you are going to take your budget to the local banker.

Another important aspect to using money is to plan for the unexpected. It is important to prepare for two or three different scenarios that may face your organization.

Do I have a budget that will fit three different scenarios, the great, the good, and the ugly?

It is important to think about what we will use monies for if we have an increase of 25 percent. How would we improve our service to our customers or to those to that we serve within our organization? It is difficult to think about, but very practical, to sketch out a budget that would be half of what we have currently. How would we go about prioritizing things? What things would need to be cut? What things are so vital that they would need to stay? This exercise can also help us use whatever funds we have. If we are going to add money to our budget we need to also ask ourselves what we should take money away from or stop doing altogether.

Although we may not think so at first, it is important to look outside the organization not only for collaborative efforts but also for people who would just like to invest in what we do. For some, this will be more difficult than for others. I am reminded of a story about the great automaker Henry Ford.

While on vacation in Dublin, Ireland, Henry Ford visited an orphanage where a building project was being planned. The director of the fund raising committee decided to call on the famous and rich Henry Ford. After their discussion, Ford judged the cause a worthy one, and he wrote out a check then and there for two thousand pounds, which was quite a gift. His generosity was so incredible that it made the headlines of the local paper. The problem was, they misquoted the figure and reported, "Ford gave twenty thousand pounds." The director of the orphanage called Henry Ford to apologize. In fact, he said, "I'll be happy to phone the director of the paper right now and correct the mistake." But feeling a little guilty, Ford said there was no need for that. With a sigh, he took out his pen and checkbook and said, "I'll give you a check for the remaining eighteen thousand pounds." But he made only one request. He said, "When the new building opens, I want this inscription on it, "I was a stranger and you took me in." (*The Little Brown Book of Antidotes*)

A fundraiser friend of mine has commented to me that there is lots of money out there, you just have to present your need to people and get them to see a vision of the impact their funds will make on your organization. If he is right, then we need to be sure and ask ourselves if there is anybody who would like to contribute or partner with us in some of the areas in which we currently have great need.

Chapter 17
Organizing Your Organization

I once read that, in a lifetime, the average American spends six weeks waiting at a red light. If that's true, then we must spend six years trying to find things we have misplaced. For one week, keep track of how much time you spend looking for things that are misplaced, or are not readily at your finger tips.

How much did disorganization cost you and your team last year?

I have built a number of teams that expressly look at how to make an office area, or a whole building, more efficient. It is amazing how many steps we could save, and how much frustration we could spare ourselves if we would just get organized. I once helped a team create a flow chart illustrating how they go about fulfilling an order for a customer. In the flow chart we found that the average processor looks at the inventory numbers for the warehouse seven times. Everyone in the group asked the obvious question why do we look at that number seven times? The answer, by another employee, was swift and brutal, "Because we can never believe it." Obviously it would save a lot of time to have the inventory counts be correct and only have to check those numbers once. Over a lifetime, that would save several leaders years of time. Whether it's getting a warehouse or your own desk organized, the following ideas can be applied to almost anything.

I find one of the best tools for organization is what is called a visual control system.

Visual Control System

A visual control system is a series of techniques used in the workplace or as a personal application to visually display information and to almost instantly know when things are in there proper place or not. Visual control systems have positive implications not only for organizing ourselves, but also for things like safety. In an emergency it's important to know quickly and without a doubt "Do I open this door or leave it shut? Do I turn this valve to the right or to the left? Should I exit this area or would it be wise to stay here?"

The Five "S"s

1. Sort
Distinguish between what is needed and what is not needed

A great technique to start this first "S" is to communicate that we are going to clean out every room and every storage cabinet and red tag any thing we think we no longer need. With a red tag on it describing what it is, the item is placed in the corner of a designated room or on a pallet for another entire week. During the second week anyone can claim something off the designated pallet—the only catch is they must give us a good reason for keeping it and the item must labeled clearly as to what it is and what it is used for. Through this method, two different organizations regained almost twenty-five percent of their storage areas. Needless junk, and things we were saving for who knows why, were discarded.

2. Stabilize
A place for every thing and everything in its place

Grandma taught us this—or at least someone should have. It's important to label every cupboard and every drawer that is in any kind of public area in our organization. These labels should be sharp and good-looking as well as clear in what they communicate. One laboratory I helped implement the visual control system in went so far as to drill holes in the back of the lab tables to put all of the computer cables through. This eliminated a lot of clutter on top of the tables. They also created a corral of tape clearly establishing a particular place for the three-hole punch and for the stapler. If you wanted to know where to find the three-holed punch, you would go to the corral labeled three-holed punch. More importantly, if you wanted to know where to return the three holed punch everyone knew where it belonged.

3. Shine
Cleaning and looking for ways to keep it clean

Every organization has created a culture when it comes to cleanliness. Some places I go into are nearly spotless and everyone seems to know it's their job to keep it that way. Other places are mired in a culture that accepts disorganization, grime, and dirt as a way of doing business. It will take some time, but you can improve the culture in your place.

4. Standardize
Maintain and Monitor the first 3S's

The habit of sorting, stabilizing, and shining needs to become the way we do business. It was reported to me that, at Disney, picking up trash is a part of every employee's job description including, Michael Eisner.

5. Sustain
Stick to the rules and reach consensus how we will deal with those who do not

A part of sticking to the rules is that we make it relatively easy to know where to dispose of things or how to organize. That's one of the secrets of a visual control system. There is a system to it and that system is obvious to everybody who works there as well as visitors. Recently, I was in the offices of a very large organization outside of Chicago. There were several thousand people in the meetings that morning. During one of the breaks, while I washed my hands in the men's restroom, I noticed that whenever there was a paper towel on the floor almost immediately somebody picked it up and threw it away. That was a silent but powerful message that the reason the place was so clean was that everybody took responsibility in keeping it that way. It had become a part of their culture.

One of the tests for a great visual control system is when a visitor can easily navigate through our buildings and around our parking lots without having to stop and ask directions every few minutes. When a visitor can easily and quickly determine where they may park, where offices are located, what areas are off limits to them, and what in areas they are welcome, then our visual control system is successful. This is also a basic principle of landscape design; proper placement of plant materials guide people through the landscape. The plants become, in essence, visual controls.

I was building teams on one college campus and suggested they have a team to improve the visual control system around campus. There were virtually no signs to tell visitors which parking lots to park in, or what was contained in six or eight buildings that were within eyeshot once they drove on campus. The team did an excellent job in labeling and putting up appropriate signs to make a first-time visitor feel right a home.

Visual control systems can be very effective in any employee area where more than one employee shares space. For instance, it's always important to be able to find the different types of paper for a copy machine. Or where the toner is kept if it runs out. Another easy place to implement visual control is in the break room. If you have a number of cabinets and drawers it wouldn't take very much effort to label each one of them with the description of the contents. When I go in for a cup of coffee I know where to find the cups, spoons, and sugar.

In today's world, with liability- related safety concerns, visual control can be a lifesaver. Where do I go in case of an emergency? One time I was walking through the back part of a factory and noticed a water hydrant was running wide open. It crossed my mind that perhaps it was intended to be running full blast, or maybe it was a mistake, or maybe it was some problem I should alert someone about. I wasn't sure what to do. Visual control would have had a sign saying, "Flushing the system" or, "If water hydrant is running notify building superintendent at number 123," and then it would point to the phone on the wall. That would be sound and prudent safety-related visual control.

We have many good examples of visual control systems. Usually, any fast food restaurant has a pretty well-established visual control system. It may be the first time I have been to that restaurant but I know exactly where to make my order, where to pick it up, where the soft drinks are, and where the trash cans are. Why? Because everything around me indicates those things. It is all visually controlled.

What is your filing system?

It has been my privilege to serve nearly two hundred people as their personal coach. Many times, leaders want to work on personal organization. I have found one of the most helpful and simple ways to help organize your information and paper work is to establish three-ring notebooks. I personally use this method in the following manner: I have a set of three ring binders that are tabbed 1-31 and have all the clients or all the projects that I am currently working on labeled on one of these tabs. I have three notebooks simply because I have three basic areas of clients. So, I divide them up according to their area plus each tab has a certain client. I refer to these notebooks four to five times a week.

I have another set of three ring binders. In this group, there are about fifteen binders and each of them is clearly labeled on the spine as well as on the front. They are set off the side of my desk on a shelf nearby. These are projects that I will probably turn to once a week.

The third wave of organization in my office is that of hanging files. These would be projects or clients that I am not working with currently or that I might only refer to once a month or less. I have suggested this to numerous leaders and many of them have responded by saying that it helps them a great deal. To help facilitate this system, I have a three hole punch right beside my desk and if I receive a fax or print out an e-mail that needs to be stored with the clients materials, I will immediately three hole punch it and put it in that notebook. I know from experience, that if I do not use this system, the paper will get lost or I will waste several minutes in frustration trying to locate the document. Another advantage I find is that if I am talking on the phone I can take my pad of paper which is already three hole punched and write notes that can be easily slipped into one of the three ring binders as soon as I am done with the conversation. This system can also easily capture sticky notes or half sheets of paper that I can tape onto a large sheet of paper or put into one of the pockets of the appropriate binder.

Do I have a written to-do list?

It is simple to have a written list that is prioritized with things that you need to accomplish for the day. I find it most productive to make sure that this list is pretty well complete the night before, so I can sleep better when my mind starts working on things in the middle of the night (though usually I find that an advantage not a nuisance). When morning comes, I know my priorities I know what I am going to work on first and the day just seems to get started on the right foot.

Do I need a calendar that works for me as well as other colleagues around me?

Many organizations find that an office calendar located prominently at the incoming desk or break room helps everyone to be basically aware of what's going on in the office. People can put their own schedules on there as to when they are going to be gone. They can mark red-letter days for inspections, or for when dignitaries are going to be in their department. It can be a very functional calendar for the whole work team. Electronic calendars are also great.

Do I have easy access to frequently used e-mails and phone numbers?

Again most of us have this already, but some kind of personal data assistant or address/phone book is almost a must. Personally, I hate looking things up in the phone book. I would much rather have it electronically stored or readily available on a list that is in a pull-out drawer on my desk. This seems to save a great deal of time and make me more likely to make the needed phone call or type the e-mails.

One of the vital things to do in organizing ourselves is to observe the 80/20 rule.

How do I spend eighty percent of my time?

The application of the 80/20 rule dictates that we spend eighty percent of our time doing those things for which we are gifted the other twenty percent of time we will need to do things we are not as comfortable with and maybe aren't as good at but still need to do. One of the important aspects of organizing ourselves well and being efficient is to use the talents of your team to the best advantage of everyone. I'm reminded that everybody is talented—just at different things. Everyone is also weak at different things. It is important to maximize what you are good at and spend most of your time doing those things. Let others in your team do what they're good at and make sure we do all we can to align our efforts.

To further illustrate my point, I'll adapt an old parable. There once was an organization that wanted to make everything fair so they decided that everyone would have to do every task. In this organization there was a duck. The duck was excellent at swimming better than any one else in the company, but he was only average at flying and was very poor at running. Because he was deficient in running, the leadership decided to enroll him in an extended running class. This caused his webbed feet to be badly worn, so that he was only average at swimming by the end of the six-week course.

Another colleague in the company was the rabbit, who was a star in his running ability but developed a nervous twitch in his leg muscles because of so much time being devoted to improving his swimming.

Another team member was the squirrel. He was excellent at climbing but encountered constant frustration and friction in a flying class because the boss made him start from the ground up instead of from treetop down like he preferred. He developed muscle cramps from over exertion, and received a letter of warning for poor marks in running.

The eagle was another outstanding member of the team, but was considered to be a problem employee with severe attitude problems. He was a nonconformist who always out-did everyone at tree climbing, but could never be convinced to do it the way every one else did it; instead, he flew up the tree.

The moral of the story is simple: each team member has their own capabilities at which they naturally excel, unless they are expected or forced to fill a mold that they don't fit. I realize that powerful leaders need to be well rounded. Some leaders need to be excellent at a multitude of skills. But there will still be things we are very good at, and we should spend more of our time doing those things for the betterment of the whole organization.

CHAPTER 18
RISK TAKING

If I were to put a board that was four inches thick and four inches wide and 25-feet long on the floor would you walk from one end to the other for a twenty-dollar bill? If I took that same board and put it on top of two chairs would you walk from one end to the other for a twenty-dollar bill? If I took that same board and put it between two 40 story buildings would you walk from one building to the other on that board for a twenty-dollar bill? All of you have heard some similar illustration before, but it illustrates a good point about assessing risk. Most people would take you up on your offer to walk across the board when it is lying on the floor. There would be very little risk and a twenty-dollar reward. Most people would also agree to your offer to walk across the board when it is only three feet off the ground, after all the risk is not too bad and still you get the twenty-dollar bill. But few would actually take the risk of walking between two 40 story buildings on that board for the same measly twenty-dollars. The difference? The difference is the risk.

It is important to take risks as a leader. It is also important to assess what the worst outcome could be and what the best outcome could be as you assess the full gambit of the risk. Sometimes you must bet the entire company on a certain course of action. Of course, it's wise to weigh all the risks as well as the potential success of any such move. Everyone takes some sort of risk. Just getting out of bed in the morning is a mild form of risk-taking. Everyone has different comfort zones when it comes to risk taking. Some can naturally handle a great deal more risk than others can.

How much risk are you willing to handle and for what purposes?

Emerson makes a good point that most people live their lives in quiet desperation. We probably don't want to end our lives knowing neither defeat nor success, only the mind-numbing neutrality of playing it safe. If we agree that we are going to take some risks in life the question becomes what am I going to risk and for what purpose?

If I am going to take a risk (especially a large risk), I want to make sure it is for a good purpose. Most people want to make a difference in the lives of people around them and at their jobs. One of those ultimate questions is:

How do you want to be remembered?

"One morning in 1888, Alfred Nobel the inventor of dynamite, the man who had spent his life amassing a fortune from the manufacture and sale of weapons, awoke to read his own obituary. The obituary was printed as the result of a simple journalistic error. Alfred's brother had died, and a French reporter carelessly reported the death of the wrong brother. Any man would be disturbed over the circumstances, but to Alfred the shock was overwhelming because he saw himself as the world saw him— "the dynamite king (the weapon maker)," the great industrialist who had made an immense fortune from explosives. This—as far as the general public was concerned—was the entire purpose of his life (so said the obituary). None of his true intentions—to break down the barriers that separated men and ideas—were recognized, or given serious consideration. He was quite simply in the eyes of the public a merchant of death, and for that alone he would be remembered...As he read his obituary with shocking horror, he resolved to make clear to the world the true meaning and purpose of his life. This would be done through the final disposition of his fortune. His last will and testament would be the expression of his life's ideals...and the result would be the most valued prizes given to this day to those who have done most for the cause of world peace—The Nobel Peace Prize."

Alfred Nobel took a risk to change how people viewed the purpose of his life. That risk paid off, many times over, as his Nobel Peace Prize has influenced and inspired millions since it was established. One of the greatest obstacles in taking any significant risk is not for yourself but probably for others around you. Almost every successful leader has many stories of people who tried to discourage them by saying "You will never make it" or "It is too dangerous."

We all know that Chuck Yeager was the first pilot to break the sound barrier; but, what is surprising to most people, is that there were a number of pilots before him who had also tried to break the sound barrier. Chuck Yeager talks about two pilots, in particular, as he reflects on the momentous event of breaking the sound barrier. One of those pilots, a few weeks before Chuck's try, had reported that as he approached the speed of sound the plane began to shake violently, the pilot panicked because of the response of the plane, so he tried to slow down which caused the plane to crash and he lost his life. A second pilot, a little more than a week later, experienced the same situation and responded the same way and he too crashed and lost his life. As Chuck Yeager approached the speed of sound, his plane also began to shake violently. His decision was to push on in what could have been the ultimate risk. His thinking was he would probably die if he let up and if he were going to die he might as well go out in a blaze of glory. Of course, what happened is this: once his plane broke through the sound barrier, things smoothed out again and he was able to safely establish the record and make it back to his base, and he became a hero. He was the first man to have "The Right Stuff."

Although few of us will ever attempt any such world record, it will feel almost the same way when we test our resolve in taking large risks. It will probably feel like we are about to break up—but that may be just the time to keep pushing onward a little longer, to push through the problems and make the risk all worthwhile. As leaders, when we take risks in the workplace or in our own personal lives there will always be the armchair quarterbacks who analyze our actions after the fact. If it fails, of course they will say well that wasn't a wise move at all. If we succeed, they will identify with us and claim that they would have done the same thing. Taking risks is a very individual thing. But it is important to take risks to whatever extent we can, study the situation and gather all the facts possible, then make a purposeful and educated choice.

On the wall of a prestigious military academy posted their "Cadet Maxim" posted. It read: **"Risk more than others think is safe. Care more than others think is wise. Dream more than others think is practical. Expect more than others think is possible."** Those are four qualities of a great leader. Educated risk-taking is an important facet of great leadership.

CHAPTER 19
INFLUENCING AND CONVINCING

Every one of us is simultaneously being influenced by others and influencing those around us. One of the paramount skills of a good leader is being able to influence others. As a leader, you certainly need to be a large influence on those that you are leading, but you need to influence your boss as well. The most important people to influence are those you are seeking to serve—your customers.

Persuading others, or being able to influence them, has fallen on difficult times. Sometimes we hear of people trying to buy influence. News headlines are constantly reminding us of people who are corrupt. They seek to influence political leaders or corporate leaders to go along with their own self-centered ideas. However, the action of influencing others into making decisions that will be of mutual benefit, and are based on good information, is a noble and important part of a leaders job.

How are people influenced?

The truthful answer is that different people are influenced by different things. One of the first things I usually do in building a team, in any organization, is to do what is called a four-factor behavior analysis. Many of you have probably experienced one of these behavior profiles. The profiles I do are very exciting and people constantly comment how much they learn about themselves, and about others around them. I jokingly sub-title this profile exercise, "Why Other People are so Weird."

People who carefully observe other people have noted—for thousands of years—that we all fall into one of four basic behavioral types. Decide with which of the following you most closely identify. Actually, we are all an infinite blend of all four of them, but you probably will identify most closely with one or two of the things that most influence people in their decision-making process.

1. Who else is using it?
Socialize Focus

Simply knowing who else is using your ideas, or using your product, initially influences many people. If they know those people or if they respect even one of the people that are using your ideas already, they will be influenced heavily to give your ideas a try. Be on the constant look-out for compliments you receive from your customers or anyone that you serve. These can be extremely valuable tools in influencing others to use your service.

As an example, a president of a large college once put in writing that I was the most effective outside resource for enabling their college to achieve a certain objective. I use that quote in all my promotional material. Likewise, I have collected several other positive comments to be a part of a whole page of college presidents and their comments on my work. This one page has great influence on prospective college presidents as they consider using my services.

Any time a customer or someone you are serving makes a positive comment, you might want to ask if you can quote them or if they would put that in writing. It is surprising how many of these comments you can accumulate over a year's time. These can become very valuable in influencing prospective customers or in influencing your boss to approve new budget expenditures.

2. What does it do and how efficient is it?
Direct or Focus Results

Others are more influenced by bottom line. They want to know what a product of service does and by when it will be ready. They are most influenced by the proof in the pudding. We can influence this type of person most by letting them use our product or service, or demonstrating it and asking them to decide for themselves. Believe me, it's more effective if they decide for themselves—they will always be influenced most heavily by bottom line results.

For these people, I point out things like how much money you can save the institution or company. Some teams have saved or produced in new revenue

$400,000.00! Even if I can't save them money, I may be able to dramatically improve the quality of their service. These types of bottom line results are very influential with people who don't care who else is using your service, but do care about the bottom line results that they can expect in their own organization.

3. How do you reach your conclusions?
Thinker Focus

These types of thinkers are most influenced by your logic. They are very interested in details and where you came up with your data. They are most influenced with your good logic. Do your arguments hold water?

One of the approaches that I insist on as I build teams in organizations, is that they work on real live processes that make a difference to the organization. I have found it counter-productive to teach the tools of constant improvement by building a better paper airplane. My logic is that we should attack real-live process problems and make a significant difference in the organization through the use of the tools and the seven step process. Good logic will influence many people.

4. How will what you are saying effect those around me?
Relator Focus

Research shows that the largest percentage of people are influenced when you can show them how what you are proposing, or what you're selling, influences them directly and those that they care about. Your influence will be improved if you can show what you do will help them and make the lives of those around them improve as well.

I am able to point out that those who are participants of the teams often comment that what they learned helped them not only on the job, but also in their personal lives and in theirs families. Many organizations are influenced to provide training that will not only help the organization but also help the personal lives of their employees. Dual purpose training has double and triple the value for the organization.

As a leader, it is important to develop influencing strategies that are long term and that cover all four of the previously mentioned behavioral types. The bottom line is, we have to be authentic. Any board of directors or boss will see through your facade if you try to butter them up two weeks before you present them with a 25 increase for your budget.

As a leader, it is important to authentically care about your crew, your team members, and your whole organization year in and year out. The authenticity of your leadership will influence them to believe the numbers and the data and the arguments that you present to them, because they will believe that you genuinely care about them.

Do you authentically believe in what you do and are you excited about your product or services?

The famous New York diamond dealer, Harry Winston, heard about a wealthy Dutch merchant who was looking for a certain kind of diamond to add to his collection. Winston called the merchant, told him that he had the perfect stone, and invited the collector to come to New York to examine it.

The collector flew to New York and Winston assigned a salesman to meet him and show him the diamond. When the salesman presented the diamond to the merchant he described the expensive stone by pointing out all its fine technical features. The merchant listened and praised the stone but turned away and said, "It's a wonderful stone but not exactly what I wanted."

Winston, who had been watching the presentation from a distance, stopped the merchant and asked, "Do you mind if I show you the diamond once again?" The merchant agreed and Winston presented the same stone but instead of talking about the technical features of the stone, Winston spoke spontaneously about his genuine admiration for the diamond and what a rare thing of beauty it was. Abruptly, the customer changed his mind and bought the diamond.

While he was waiting for the diamond to be packaged and be brought to him, the merchant turned to Winston and asked, "Why did I buy it from you when I had no difficulty saying no to your salesman?"

Winston replied, "The salesman is one of the best men in the business, and he knows more about diamonds than I do. I pay him a good salary for what he knows. But I would gladly pay him twice as much if I could put into him something that I have that he lacks. You see he, knows diamonds, but I love them."

This story illustrates one of the single greatest principals of influence: people are far more influenced by the depths of your beliefs and emotions than any amount of logic or knowledge you possess. (Michael LeBoeuf, *How to Win Customers and Keep them for Life*)

One of the most important things to aid our influence and improve our ability to convince and persuade, is the not-so-simple act of being prepared. It is extremely important to do your homework. I have the privilege of serving on many task forces. Those who have the most influence, often are those who come well prepared. People listen to the team member who has done her homework and comes with data, quotations, charts, and clear ideas. All too often, the majority of committee members show up at a meeting, open their file and only *then* begin to focus on the points on the agenda.

Homework, as we all know, can be time consuming and difficult. Good leaders do not try to be experts on everything. Periodically, it is important to select the vital *few things* that will be your center of influence.

CHAPTER 20
FEEDBACK

Feedback is a two-way street involving both the giving and the receiving of feedback. As a leader, you will need to receive feedback from those whom you are leading, your co-leaders, and your boss. The same thing is true of giving feedback; you will want to give feedback to the same three pools of people. This chapter will be focused on *giving* feedback but it is just as important to be good at receiving feedback.

If you are not getting the information or the feedback that you need, it is important to ask for the appropriate information, data, and feedback. Without good and frequent feedback it is impossible to stay on course. As you drive down the street, your eyes, ears, and all of your senses are constantly giving you thousands of bits of feedback. You use this feedback to stay your course. That feedback helps you to stay on the road, avoid obstacles, make constant course corrections, and make hundreds of judgment calls pertaining to your progress. If we need constant feedback to accomplish a fairly simple objective—like driving down the street—we certainly need lots of feedback in order to achieve the various objectives in our organization.

Have we agreed upon the target?

If at all possible, it is helpful that your entire team understands and gains ownership of your target. One of the best ways to get everyone to feel a sense of ownership is to have everybody involved in setting the target. I often advise leaders to come up with the two or three essentials that are part of the target and are not up for compromise. Then, invite the participation of everyone on the team in clearly defining and clearly setting the goals.

"If the ship misses the harbor it is seldom the harbor's fault." If we miss our targets, it is usually because we were not clear about where we were going.

Is the target stable?

A number of years ago, I worked with the leaders of a very large national company. One of the challenges I sought to help them solve was the problem with their targeted goals. The good news was that they had specific numbers and specific targets. The really bad news was that those targets and those numbers changed every quarter. Divisional leaders never knew what the next quarter would bring. It is very difficult to mount a significant campaign to overcome problems if the goal line and rules of the game are changed every ninety days.

Yes, often we are called upon to hit a moving target. Our customers are not standing still. Their needs and their expectations are ever-changing. The point is that we need to clearly establish who our customers are, or whom we are trying to serve, and how we can best take aim at their needs and their expectations. If I go pheasant hunting, I do not know which way the pheasant will fly. It may go to the right or to the left or straight ahead, but I will always be aiming at a pheasant. It will be in that sense a stable target. I will never be tempted to aim at the dog, or shoot at a tin can, or aim at a fence post. I am pheasant hunting, so that's the target. In that pursuit, I can constantly gain feedback about my shooting and the results. I can check my strategy and get feedback on the equipment I am using. I don't want to use a B-B gun to hunt pheasant, nor do I need an elephant gun.

Am I providing all the resources possible to remove obstacles?

As a leader, I want to provide feedback and resources to my team that will help them overcome obstacles. There will always be hurdles in our path but many times the team is stymied because they don't know the proper resources that will help them to overcome the problem.

Am I providing personal and team encouragement?

It is important to give a wide variety of feedback. Of course, we need to give negative feedback if we are missing the mark and if things are going poorly. Usually systems are already very good at giving negative feedback.

It is extremely important to give positive encouragement. As a leader, it means a great deal to your team to sense that you are authentically on their side. It is also important as a leader to give individual and team encouragement. Catch someone doing something right and praise them for it. Positive reinforcement is a strong motivator.

When one of my sons was young and involved in the YMCA basketball league, I was his coach. He and his teammates were only in third and fourth grade but already very enthusiastic about the game of basketball. Even at that age they knew the basic objective was to put the ball in the hoop. I would be playing the role of a judge if after every shot I told my players whether they made it or not. This is needless feedback and not helpful. If my son takes a shot and he misses it, and I—in anger—levitate off the bench and scream, "You missed it!" then I have added nothing to his knowledge base.

If, however, I play the role of a good coach, I might call a time-out. Upon doing this, I would give him some feedback that might sound like this: "If you tuck in your elbow, and keep it closer to your body, and flip your wrist a little more, the ball will go in more often." Now I am *coaching* and giving some profitable feedback. Even in third grade he knew he missed the objective—his question was "How do I make it next time?" Your employees will want to know the same thing, as it pertains to their problems.

Many leaders state the obvious negative feedback concerning missed goals. In all probability, your team already knows that they have missed the mark. Encouragement and feedback, or reflection about what might work better next time, is what is needed most.

What kind of feedback does your team need?

What facts, figures, or data does your team need? Some of this data might already be available, but is just not delivered to them. What data is not available and is currently not being collected, but needs to be collected?

What is the most efficient way to collect data? How much information is needed? Do we need to collect this data hourly, daily, weekly, monthly, or once a year? Some organizations have feedback for their employees at every opportunity they can get information describing outcomes.

Do we agree on the operational definition of things?

Don't overlook the need to operationally define some terms. To operationally define means to define terms in words that are meaningful to your organization. We all know about Webster's definition, the operational definition is how your organization uses that term.

For instance, I have worked with several long term care facilities. One of the key pieces of information that they gather every month is the number of falls that are experienced by residents in their care. Obviously no one wants anyone at long-term care facility to have a fall. We have found that employees and leaders define the word "fall" differently. This phenomena became especially noticeable toward the end of some months. If there were a large number of falls that had already been reported, people tended to get creative in what they determined was a fall. The employees reasoned that they didn't want to get in trouble for too many falls. The result was that some "falls" were described as a "slip."

In another organization that specialized in making phone calls to potential clients we carefully counted the number of phone calls made each hour. The company then established a quota for its' employees. Each employee needed to make his or her quota of calls each hour. As some employees neared the end of each hour they would check the number of calls they had made. Now, if it wasn't going to meet the quota, then they would call one another and hang up! This would register a call on their data sheet., but this is not exactly what leadership intended to happen. What we need here is an operational definition of the term "call." Perhaps an even better idea is to engage the employees in establishing reasonable quotas and to create a very clear operational definition of what an "effective call" might sound like.

How am I doing?

Every leader and every employee has this basic question on their mind: "How am I doing?" Actually we want this answer four different ways. First, I must access for myself, how I am doing. Second it is important to get the perspective of my boss in regard to my performance. The third perspective, is extremely important and perhaps the most important of all: "How does my customer think I am doing?" The fourth perspective is "how do my co-workers view my performance?"

Get data and feedback on all three perspectives. It may not be easy, but it is important in order to make course corrections and make improvements. It is also extremely important to get this kind of feedback often, not just once a year.

How can I picture the feedback?

Many times it is much more useful and meaningful to everyone if we can somehow picture the feedback by way of charts. Charts such as Pareto Charts or Run Charts are very effective in helping people quickly visualize what is happening in the workplace. Also, literal pictures of outcomes, things we want to avoid, or things we want to repeat are important to include in the feedback system.

I remember one manufacturing company that had two large display boards. The one on the left was filled with examples of bad product that had been produced at the plant. On the right were examples of good product that everyone was striving to produce. Each day as workers went in and out of the break room they could take note of both boards. It is one good way to provide visual feedback.

Am I showing the connection between feedback and decision making?

It is extremely important to show a connection between the feedback you are receiving and the decisions that are being made in the organization. Good, consistent feedback ought to help us make better decisions. The other reason to clearly show the connection between feedback and decisions, is to show that the system is working. We are using the information or feedback in the decision-making process. After all, if you ask me to provide feedback to you and I don't see you ever using it, it won't take long for me to stop giving you that feedback.

Chapter 21
Got Dreams?

Nearly every great change or great enterprise starts with a dream. A dream is a vision or a view of what something will be like before it exists.

Ask almost any child what they want to be when they grow up, and they will usually have a ready answer. I want to be an athlete, a fireman, a judge, a teacher, or any one of a hundred other things that they have as a dream. As we get older and become adults, there is a common tragedy that can afflict us all. That tragedy is that we lose our ability to dream. There is some reason for the loss of our dreams in adulthood. After all, as children it seemed quite straightforward to want to become a doctor. As we got older we learned all the demands and requirements that would have to be met for us to become a doctor, and we began to see the dream fade. But some of those dreams persisted, and probably still influence us today. As a leader, it is extremely important that you still have the ability to see your organization for what it can be, and not just for its current situation.

In 1963, Dr. Martin Luther King Jr. made his historical speech from the steps of the Lincoln Memorial in Washington DC in front of 250,000 people, with millions more watching via television. The name of that speech was "I Have a Dream." You have to admit, it might have lost something if his speech had been entitled "I Have a Strategic Plan."

Now, there is nothing wrong with having a strategic plan. We will take that up in the next chapter. But before we can have plans, we need to have some clear dream of where we are going. A number of years ago, I was a participant involved in a seminar on clarifying of your dreams. By the way, when I say vision or dreams I am not talking about anything psychic. I am simply talking about a clear picture in our minds of what we want to become, or what we want our organizations to become. During the training, the facilitator instructed us all to take a large sheet of paper and about a dozen crayons. He then instructed us all to sit on the floor, like when we were kids, and over the next twenty minutes draw a clear picture of our dreams for our own personal future. I'm probably like most of you. At first I thought this was an exceedingly dumb exercise. But, I saw other people doing it so I thought I better try. Although I am not very good at drawing, I will never forget the image that soon developed on the paper before me. That picture serves as a "North Star" for my plans even to this day.

Do I have a clear picture of my dreams?

It is important to spend some time clarifying what is important to you. It is important to clarify our dreams.

Do I have a clear picture of my employee's dreams?

It can be very helpful to the whole organization to spend a little time clarifying the dreams of our employees. What are their dreams for the organization? How do they see its future? How do they see their part in the organization over the next two to three years?

Is my dream the first step toward reality?

It is true that dreams need to have some chance of becoming reality. I might dream of saving the world from outer space aliens that are invading our planet. However, hopefully this is not rooted in any form of reality. Making plans to pull off such a dream would be a waste of time. It is important to strike some sort of balance between the type of dream that is going to stretch us, and the type of dream that will be fruitless and foolish. It is important to err on the side of dreaming big dreams.

Can I make significant progress in our organization without a clear-shared mental picture of where we are headed?

The bottom line is, it seems unlikely that we will make significant progress if we do not have a clear mental picture of where we are going. Other people in our organization need to share the same mental picture. A team where every member shares a clear mental picture of having a championship year is much more likely to reach the playoffs than a team that only shares the dream of making it through the season.

Do you dream big dreams?

Chapter 22
Strategic Planning

Strategic planning is the kind of planning that takes place on a large all-inclusive scale and over a long-term period. The roots of strategy are often found in military applications. The strategic plan includes all the aspects of confronting an enemy over a sustained period of time. For instance, if I were a general and my plan was to go in there and blast them, that would not be a good example of strategic planning. Many battles and wars have been lost not because of lack of a plan on the front lines but because of insufficient planning to provide for continuous supply of essentials like water, food, communications, re-supply of arms, medical treatment, and sufficient rest.

As a leader, you are probably part of a strategic plan. If you are the top leader, you need to be the initiator and sustainer of such a plan. It is one thing to have a dream, it is quite another thing to put timelines and all the necessary preparations together to cause that dream to become a reality.

What are the key elements to your strategic plan?

Processes are the building blocks of any strategic plan. Within every process there are five main ingredients.

1. People
2. Environment
3. Materials
4. Machinery
5. Methods

In your strategic plan, have you aligned these five things over a long period of time with your over-all dream? The strategic plan should begin to answer questions like who is going to accomplish the dream? What kind of training do they need? What kind of skills will be required of them? How will they be organized?

The environment part of the strategic plan has to do with everything from the culture and values we establish to the physical environment that will be confronted by the workforce. If we are expecting peak performance from our workers in a work environment that is too hot, cold, bright, dark, dusty, or unsafe, then we will have an incomplete or faulty strategic plan.

Every strategic plan must consider the 3 "M"s, what **machinery** or equipment will be need, what **materials** are necessary, and what **methods** will be employed.

Another essential part of the strategic plan, is an assessment of our competition. Often, we recognize that we are in a race with others providing the same product or services. Those that we wish to serve have other choices to meet their needs. A good strategic plan honestly and objectively accesses where we are in the race, and the strengths and weaknesses of our competition. Don't neglect the possibility of cooperating with your competition.

Other areas to consider, are the forces that are out of our control and yet may have a profound influence on our organization. One example would be the world economy. We can not control the value of the dollar compared to the yen. We can not control every aspect of worldwide inflation. We will need to have a plan of how to react to large changes or potential changes that are taking place around us. As we mentioned in chapter two, a good strategic plan and a good leader anticipates the future and prepares for its challenges. Many organizations have found it helpful to develop a strategic plan that would fit any of three or four scenarios. The strategies will differ depending on what scenario we envision.

Are we prepared for the long haul?

Are we able to sustain our efforts over a long period of time? Ten years ago, for the first time, I came face to face with a company that actually had a hundred year plan for dominating their particular market place. My first thought was, "They can't be serious!?" My second thought was, if they are serious then we're in trouble. The actual value of a hundred year plan can be debated. But it certainly has much positive strength as it tries to forecast the challenges of an entire century. It is certainly much better than the organization that only has a 90-day vision for the future.

Granted, in a fast-changing world it is difficult to envision—with much clarity—the situation we may be confronted with three years from now, let alone one hundred years. But it is more foolish to fly by the seat of our pants from year to year without any thought of the long-term implications of the decisions we are making. Think long-term in the strategic plan.

Here is one method to deploy a strategic plan:

Strategic Planning

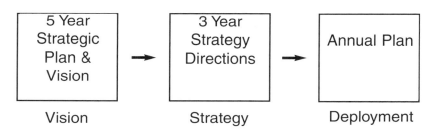

Chapter 23
Goal Setting

In the leadership development training I conduct, I often ask participants if they regularly write down specific goals. From this informal research I have concluded that over 90 percent do not regularly write down specific goals.

The next question I ask is, "Why don't most people write down specific goals?" The number one answer is **fear of failure.** Written goals are like two sides of a coin. If I write down goals, and I do not achieve those goals, it seems to make our failure that much more painful. However, goals that are written down and achieved create an even more encouraging sense of satisfaction.

It is important to face the fear of written goals head-on . There are two things to keep in mind. Number one: it's ok to fail. In one sense it's ok to fail, in another sense none of us wants to fail—even though it's an inevitable part of life. Everybody that I have met or read about that seems to be wildly successful has had some deep failures in their life.

The second thing to remember, is that even in failing we learn from the failure. So, lets not take ourselves quite so seriously and be willing to write down goals and be clear about what we would like to achieve as an individual and as an organization.

I am a strong advocate of each person in an organization having a personal improvement plan. With the support and encouragement of another leader or our boss, each individual establishes at least one personal improvement goal at least every three to six months. Usually, I'm not too fussy about what the goals are if they relate to the overall mission of the organization and how that individual is going to personally expand their skill set or their knowledge.

In 1979, I was challenged to develop my own personal dream list. (See "Principals of Dreaming" in chapter 21). The speaker instructed us to take an hour or two and just sit down and write all the things we would like to do, or be, or have, on a dream list. It is important to have no holds barring you—and don't worry if you can afford it, or if you are young or old enough, just write down your dream list.

I took up the challenge and compiled a list that contained 56 items. Over the past 20 years I have seen over half those dreams become reality!

After you establish your dream list, it is important to place your dreams into categories. You may want to use the eight areas of life that were suggested in chapter four. In fact, to help your dream list along you might want to write down each of those eight areas and try to jot down at least five dreams in each area. The areas are:

1. Spiritual Health

2. Mental Health

3. Physical Health

4. Financial Health

5. Marriage and or Family

6. Friends

7. Vocation

8. Life Purpose and plan

Many people enjoy adding the category "Hobbies."

Once the dream list is established and categorized, the next step is to prioritize each of the items in each of the categories. Beyond that, you may want to prioritize the winners in each category and come up with the one or two biggest priorities in your life.

In my own experience, the 56 things in my dream list probably would have taken me about 300 years to achieve. Because I don't plan on living 300 years, I needed to prioritize and come up with the things that I really *really* wanted to accomplish in my lifetime. Once the items are prioritized, then we need to set specific goals.

Dreams without a timeline remain dreams. I have already advocated the act of dreaming. But, it is essential to take some of those dreams that are the highest priority to us, and set timelines and goals for those high priority dreams. Failure to do this will result in procrastination.

One of the many advantages of setting specific goals is that it helps deliver us from the tyranny of the urgent. Often we get caught up in the minute details of life and miss our big purpose and our goals. Writing down specific goals helps lead us to accomplishing tasks that will lead us to successfully reaching goals. Successfully reached goals will help us achieve our overall purpose.

One acronym that is often used in goal setting is "Smart goals." The five terms aligned with the word **smart** are important ones to remember in relationship to setting goals. However, I'd like to suggest that we set **"Smarter goals."**

1. **S-specific: The more detail, the more I can begin to see this goal start to take place.**

2. **M-measurable: How will I measure success? It's important to have two or more measurements to keep us in balance. I may want to measure speed and accuracy because I don't want to make more mistakes.**

3. **A-attainable: Is the goal realistic? Is it attainable in the required time?**

4. **R-resourced: Have I adequately planned the needed resources, things like people, machinery, and training.**

5. **T-time framed: Have I established a timeline? (A good tool here is a Gantt chart.)**

6. **E-energized: Am I properly motivated? Does the whole team feel a sense of urgency and energy to accomplish this goal? Have I clearly answered the question "Why"? Have I clearly outlined the proper motivation?**

7. **R-related: Is this goal owned by everybody? Is it our baby or is it someone else's child? Also, is the goal related to our overall purpose?**

As you set future goals, it may be helpful to use the **Smarter Goals** as a checklist for writing better goals. You may also want to suggest it to the rest of your team. Perhaps it could become part of the culture in your organization.

Following is one further thing to think about concerning goals. I think it is important, as you set significant goals, to also establish a time when you are going to celebrate. Perhaps your goal is to renovate a building, or landscape ten acres, or install new software. Whatever the goal may be, it is important to establish when it is that we will celebrate. This will often serve as another motivator toward completing the tasks.

My father served as a state senator in Iowa for 24 years. I can remember, at the beginning of each campaign, he would make a special point of setting a date to celebrate. For all those who volunteered to make the campaign a success, it was an important day of recognition and celebration.

CHAPTER 24
PRIORITIZING

Frozen with busyness! Do you remember the old time variety shows where some guy is busily spinning plates on wobbly poles? The entertainment value increased as he spun more and more plates, on more and more wobbly poles. We all wondered when one of them would fall off. It may have been entertaining on a variety show, but it's no way to live your life.

For many of us, we get too many plates spinning and it causes us to become frozen in the busyness of trying to keep what we have going—plus one more thing. In our heart of hearts, we know something is going to fall, so why continue the rat race? We give up because of a lack of focus.

The fact of the matter is, we cannot do everything—we must *prioritize!* Part of prioritizing is deciding what we are **not** going to do.

Have you decided in what areas you are going to fail?

A wise president of an organization shared with me that part of the formula for success is deciding where your going to fail. For instance, at this point in my life I have decided not to be an avid skier. There is nothing wrong with skiing, I even enjoy skiing. But, skiing is one of many things that I have decided to allot little or no time for in my schedule. Why? So I can have time to do other things well.

What one thing are you going to master?

Certainly, it is possible to master more than one thing but one is where we all need to start. We have all heard the truism "a jack of all trades, a master of none." It is my understanding that what Benjamin Franklin was really encouraging us to do is to be a jack of all trades and a master of **one**.

In the very demanding field of leadership, it is important in one sense to be a jack of all trades. We need to be proficient at many things to be a good leader. But it is also true that the most effective leaders seem to have prioritized a very small number of things that they have mastered. I have had the privilege of coaching a number of leaders and I have always encouraged them to boil their priorities down to a list of the **vital few.** By vital few I mean five or less things they need to focus on every day. These would be the five or less things that are extremely vital to their vocation or their particular goals. Every day will be filled with competing priorities, but the **vital few** must seldom be bumped from the top of the priority list. The **vital few** must be focused on each day. If something must suffer, it should not be the **vital few.**

> **"I soon learned to scent out that which was able to lead to the fundamentals and to turn aside everything else, from the multitude of things that clutter up the mind and divert it from the essential."**
> (Albert Einstein)

Those leaders that are mediocre are spending time deciding between good and bad. Excellent leaders are spending time deciding between what is good and what is excellent. Leaders need to spend 80 percent of their time pursuing those **vital few** that are excellent and will lead them to the highest outcomes.

This skill of prioritizing and focusing on a vital few things is something that I have wrestled with for many years. Often, I have lost the wrestling match. I have many interests and many things at which I would like to become proficient. But again and again I admire people who have focused on a small number of things, or on one thing for which they have decided to become the best in the class. Therefore, each year I try to sharpen the point of my life. To hone in on a vital few things in which I will become excellent.

For what shall I become single minded?

On my desk is a large glass vessel filled with 304 red stones. Next week, it will contain only 303 stones. It is my way of vividly reminding myself of how many weeks until I turn fifty-five. It reminds me that I have 300 Saturdays until then. Three hundred Mondays three hundred Sundays—you get the idea. I want to make each week count. My original thought was, I might try to retire or at least shift gears at age 55. The way the stock market has been going, I may just throw in 300 more stones and keep going!

The key thing is to spend time every week focusing on priorities. Some priorities are not urgent; that is, they can be put off all too often. Priorities like making memories with your family or taking care of your own personal health can often get shoved aside in the business of life. Then, before you know it, there are only a few months or a few years left, and we are reaping the consequences of putting things off that actually were of high priority for us.

Each year it is a great idea to ask yourself some of the following questions:

> What is my greatest strength as a person?
> What does that unique strength tell me about my purpose in life?
> What single thing would I do this year if it were all that I could get done?
> Where would I like to visit this year?
> What is the biggest barrier that holds me back and how can I begin to overcome it this year?
> What single habit would I most like to break this year?
> What single habit would I most like to establish this year?
> What single person or small group of people would I most like to build up, develop, and coach this year?
> What group of "pros" can I learn from this year?
> What one thing can I do this year to better hone my life to a sharper focus?

Chapter 25
Delegating

To delegate means to entrust to another some of your authority. Leaders sometimes hand out responsibility without also handing out the needed authority. Responsibility without authority puts the employee in a bind. He or she has the responsibility to carry out a function but does not have the appropriate authority to solve problems in connection with carrying out that function.

A leader might delegate the responsibility for setting up a work schedule for employees. Inevitably, that responsibility will involve making decisions regarding employees who call in sick or who are late to work. Without the appropriate authority to take action and remedy problem situations, the one entrusted with scheduling can be put in a double bind. One bind is, they can't solve the problems, the other bind is that they are held responsible for the problems.

Some leaders are very capable, intelligent people, but are not able to effectively entrust others with part of the leadership load. This inability will often lead those leaders to early burnout.

Do you have the ability to build a good staff around you?

The ability to multiply one's self is an essential skill for any leader to master. How can you mobilize others, therefore multiplying your leadership effectiveness? Good delegation is like good team building. The leader tries to find the appropriate strength within the team that will fit the task. The leader then appropriately assigns staff to their areas of strength.

Do you have a written picture of what needs to be done?

Sometimes we are hesitant to delegate because it is difficult to make the hand-off of responsibilities to another person. Part of the reason that it is difficult to make the hand-off is because we have never clearly documented what we do. It is a good habit to put together a job file. Job files can be put together for every significant job within an organization. For instance, what is the job of a crew leader—what do they do? What decisions do they make? What machinery or equipment are they responsible for? How do they fit into the leadership scheme in the organization? Who do they answer to, and who answers to them? The answers to these questions can begin the makeup of a good job folder. Other details like phone numbers, addresses, and e-mails of important people are resources that can be included in the job file.

A good yearlong calendar of events is important in most job folders. Things like deadlines for reports, or when to start certain projects can be very helpful to somebody coming into a new job. I once carefully looked through a job folder in which the previous employee even had lists of people who were or were not helpful to that particular department.

Could a flow chart be useful?

A very important tool that is easy to understand, but more difficult to build than you might think, is a flow chart. Flow charts simply picture step-by-step the process. Good flow charts can answer many questions and aid in your ability to hand off projects.

Does the employee know the purpose of the job?

Until we know why we are doing something, we really don't know how to do the job. For instance, if I were to delegate the task of washing the table in a training room, how would you do the job?

I have asked this very question in many seminars. The common response is, "Well I'd take a damp cloth and wipe it off." That is a perfectly logical and good answer. However, if I were to continue the instructions and tell you the purpose for washing the table, it would help you know how to do your job. For instance, if I said, "Please wash this table because tonight I'm going to take apart a lawn mower engine on the table and show a group of boy scouts how a small engine works." How would you wash the table knowing the purpose of the job? Most people respond, "Well it's already good enough," or "I might even cover it with some cardboard." They are right. They know how to wash the table now.

If I were to ask someone to wash the table and I said the purpose of the job was that their family and my family are going to have dinner on that table this evening—but the only problem is, we don't have any plates. How would you wash it knowing that purpose? Most people respond, "I would wash it very well with soap and water and make sure the soap was the kind that would kill germs and disinfect the table top." Again, now they know how to do their job! One more time I might ask you to wash that table but this time the purpose is to have your doctor take out your appendix on that table tonight. How would you wash the table now? You might call the local hospital and ask them how they get their operating rooms clean enough to prevent infection. The point is, once we know the purpose of a job we know a lot more about how to do the job. It is important to remember this principle when we are delegating.

Have you communicated the scope of the employee's authority?

In delegating, it is important to draw some boundaries around the scope of authority. The scope of the authority would include things like a timeline. The scope would include when the project must be done, and the details relating to bringing other people into the group in order to accomplish the project in a short amount of time. If there is material to obtain, or machinery to line up? What authority do they have to buy or to rent?

Another part of the scope is to determine what training might be needed in order to equip the employee to carry out the task. Do they have the authority to ask others to help with the training?

As a leader, you might go through those six servants of planning, **who, what, when, where, how,** and **why,** as you describe the scope of responsibility to the employee. Clearly defining the scope can prevent lots of problems and lots of hard feelings. Don't forget to include in your instructions what kind of feedback you want from your employee. When do you want them to check back with you with progress reports? And last, but not least, what are the consequences to the organization (and maybe to the employee) if this delegated task is not completed on time?

The very nature of supervising others is to have, "Super-vision." As a leader, it is your job to stand on the hilltop while viewing the whole field, so you can better access the big picture. Lead others in accomplishing the big picture, but leave the details to those who are often more competent and closer to the front lines. For instance, it is probably best to delegate to someone else the first draft of a weekly work schedule. As a leader, you can review those plans and make adjustments based on your knowledge of the big picture.

Delegation is one of those skills that can literally make or break a leader. Doing too much of the work yourself can take your eye off the big picture, and it can cause you to burn out. As you sense times of burnout developing in your own life, ask yourself, "What can I delegate to others?" The work will often get done and done well. The great thing is, you will live to lead another day.

CHAPTER 26
MOTIVATION OF THE ORGANIZATION

Motivation is achieved as a result of need or desire. The needs that we have **push** our motivation into action and our desires or dreams **pull** us toward motivated action. All people have needs and desires, so it follows that all of us are motivated.

Everyone has the basic needs of food, clothing, shelter, and safety. The jobs we offer may meet those basic needs. So, we might have the push of motivation already in action. However, to take the next step into the higher motivation that we need from our employees and ourselves, we need to capture the pull or magnetism of dreams. I mean, the dreams of significance, and the desire to make a difference in life. The kind of motivation that comes from the leadership that says, "While we are making a living with our organization, why don't we also become the best campus in the state or the best golf course in the region." Now employees are on a team that is making a living and making a life long difference to those they serve. This will make the long hours have more meaning and provide pride in work. This motivation gets inside us all. It pulls us into willingly giving that self-motivated, 110 percent that no one could ever force out of us.

One of the most memorable examples of powerful motivation took place my junior and senior years of High School. My High School was great. Of course, it was the only High School I had experienced, so it was the best one I knew. It was small, and everyone could be involved in just about whatever sport they wanted. We often had winning seasons, and we had faithful fans. Although we managed a respectable number of winning seasons, no team in any sport could claim to dominate anything. A new coach my junior year motivated us to change that attitude. He was known, and some what feared, for his emphasis on conditioning. But what I remember most is his mastery of motivation.

By my senior year, it was our clear and heartfelt goal to win every football game that season. I remember clearly how he pointed out that no one expected us to do it, and that no one in our little community had ever done it before. But, if we set our sights on an undefeated season, and played one game at a time, he knew we could do what no one had ever done before us.

As we approached another undefeated team midway through the season, we knew this game would likely decide the conference championship. They were bigger then us at almost every position. Every game had its own motivational build up, but I especially remember our coach's words before this one. He said, "Very few people ever get a chance to play on an undefeated team, this is a once in a life time shot, let's put everything we've got on the field tonight!" We won the game 14 to 8! We went on to win every game. I have been on other very successful teams, but coach was right—we never had another season in which we were undefeated. Over 30 years later, people still talk about that season in my hometown. Although, more and more it's only at our class reunions that we relive every game, play by play.

Motivating others is built on understanding others and operating under some correct insights as to how people think in their hearts. Here are five key insights:

1. People normally do what aids them in meeting their needs and dreams.

It can be that people get caught up in lose-lose behavior, i.e. they do things that harm themselves as well as those around them. But normally, if we can align the needs of our organization with the needs of our team members, they will see the win-win nature of the alignment and be highly motivated.

2. Most people want to succeed at work.

How many people do you know that come to work and as they stroll across the parking lot they say to themselves, "Hmmm, I wonder how I can mess it up today?" I know, I know, you may have someone you're suspicious of on this question, but seriously, I don't know of anyone who comes to work and wants to fail. Most people want to be a success at work. In other chapters, we have explored the fact that—most of the time—the cause of failure is more in the system that we work in than in the person's unwillingness to succeed.

3. We all want to make a difference.

As a child most of us probably had our fantasy of wanting to be Superman or Superwoman. Why? Well, besides being able to do all sorts of cool things that no one else could manage, I think the satisfaction of being a superhero is wrapped up in "making a difference in life." Think of it, Superman got to save the whole world in every half-hour episode! He made a difference! Granted, we may not be able to save the world, but people want to make a difference in their corner of their world.

4. We all have strengths and weaknesses, build on people's Strengths.

Our strengths are like rich soil that will support growth; in this case, personal growth. Weaknesses are what we are NOT... like the thin air atop a high mountain, we can't grow in the thin air of our weaknesses. Take the time and the care to find, to recognize, and to build on people's strengths. This behavior always communicates they are winners and so are you.

5. We all need and grow with authentic encouragement.

There were three players on our championship team that were recognized as First Team All State. I wasn't one of them, but our coach always communicated how important each one of us was to the team's success. He communicated his encouragement in front of others, as well as when no one else was observing. Everyone felt like they were on the All State Team.

As leaders, we can mess this entire process up any number of ways. Some societies and organizations try to guarantee everyone a job no matter what. This results in little attention being paid to quality, high productivity, and market demands. Others have been so demanding that leadership is never satisfied. This culture leads to people taking the logical action of giving up. Since there is no chance of pleasing the boss, and no reward for trying to do so, it makes sense to stop the futile attempts.

Clear, meaningful, and respected goals are the keys to a motivated individual and a motivated work force. Every work leader I know wants their team to be motivated and to have great discipline. The key to motivated teams at our organizations is understanding how our organizational goals can dovetail with the personal goals of all.

Most people want to make a difference and be involved in work that is relevant. Most people want respect, respect for their work and respect for their person. Most people want a good relationship or friendship at work.

Chapter 27
Recruiting and Outsourcing

Obtaining and keeping the right people or the right resources for your organization is paramount for achieving success. Recruiting is only the tip of the iceberg. It is also extremely important to retain quality employees.

It is important to see the big picture and have a long-term view of recruiting. Recruiting can be viewed from two extremes. The first extreme is a very positive one involving that big picture and long-term view; it is the idea of building a long-term team or a dynasty. The other extreme is simply filling slots. Sometimes it seems the only prerequisite to employment is whether the potential employee fogs a mirror.

A fully developed view of recruiting and outsourcing has at least five parts. Each part could represent 20 percent of the job of recruiting.

1. Develop a clear job description.   1 2 3 4 5

2. Recruit from dependable pools of candidates.   1 2 3 4 5

3. Train and orient the new employee.   1 2 3 4 5

4. Retain the employee through a quality culture.   1 2 3 4 5

5. Develop a network of internal and external pools of potential future employees.   1 2 3 4 5

In each of the five parts of recruiting: how is your organization doing? Take a moment and rate yourself on a scale from one to five. One being terrible and five being excellent. Being terrible at any one of the five can start to unravel the chain reaction that will produce good recruiting.

Nearly every time there is an opening in the workforce, it maybe a good time to at least briefly examine if there is anything we can stop doing. By this I mean that sometimes changes in our market, or changes in how we do things, merit examining our systems to see if there is anything that we should stop. Maybe there are some things that are no longer of value to our customer. Those are things we could stop doing without losing the favor of our customer. The self-serve gas station is a prime example of such a move.

Once we have made sure we are doing the right things and need the employee, it is important to develop a clear job description. Someone needs to be able to clearly outline exactly what the job is that we are trying to fill.

In the second stage of recruiting is to ask important questions. The fact is that what the potential employee wants, and what the employer wants, can often be worlds apart. But, we won't know this until we ask good questions. Needless to say, we probably won't get any applicants if we don't advertise or somehow communicate that a position is open. In that communication, include a short description of what the job entails. In the communication, it is important to include the things that are required of the job applicants. If they need to be able to lift 70 pounds, then it should be clearly stated up front. If there is drug screening for every applicant it is important to put it in the communication. One company that I have consulted with for several years saw a marked improvement in the pool of candidates simply by doing drug screening. Another important part of the communication is the pay range. Nearly every potential candidate will want to know, at least generally, what the job pays.

It is important to check references. The references that the potential employee lists will give a testimonial as to their character, and how people see them performing in your situation. It may also be helpful to have testimonials from your own team about the advantages of working at your place. Authentic comments from people on your staff can be a magnet that attracts others to your organization.

The third important step in recruitment is training. Good orientation in the first two or three days, and good initial training, go along way to preventing repeating the hiring process again and again. In one organization we had a team work on improving the retention rate in the company. We found that training was the number one cause of turn over. I should say, of course, that <u>a lack</u> of training was the number one cause of turnover. The team found that the typical training consisted of starting the employee on the third shift, introducing them to their supervisor, the break room, the restrooms, and their workstation. That was the extent of their training. Most employees felt overwhelmed and made the decision to quit the company within the first two weeks. The team developed trainers who were knowledgeable as well as people-friendly. These trainers, along with the team, developed a two-week program for initial orientation and initial training. Following the two weeks, the employees could opt into other training and expand their skill levels. This one change significantly improved the retention rate for the company.

Step number four is to retain. I have found that the biggest help in retaining employees is to build a positive culture. Building a positive culture for peak performance is not an easy task but it can be accomplished. Make sure your new employees spend lots of time with positive people on your staff. Warn them of some lingering negative people, and steer them away from their cynicism. Encourage them to be a part of the new culture and the new way of creating a better workplace.

The fifth part of recruitment is to develop an even stronger pool of candidates. One resource should be those employees that are already in your workforce. From there, developing a network of trust with colleges or employment agencies or temp agencies will prove helpful to consistently getting good employees.

Would it be better for the organization to outsource the work?

This certainly can be a controversial question. However, it is one worth asking. Some organizations have found that many headaches and productivity problems have gone away by simply outsourcing some of their needs. Granted, this is not the solution in every case. But it can be a resource of very talented and specialized workers that will actually save you money and improve productivity. A proper fit in your organization can also improve customer service.

Would Temp Agency Services make sense?

Some organizations have certain jobs that have nearly 100 percent turnover. For these particular jobs, it may be wise to go with the flow and use the services of a temp agency. Obviously, these jobs must be ones that an employee can be trained to do in an extremely short amount of time. Provide good supervision for them. The point is, if there is going to be lots of turnover, let a temp agency care for the recruitment problem. Another advantage is that you can find great employees that mesh with your team by way of using them through a temp agency first.

Chapter 28
Building People

One of the greatest satisfactions any leader can experience is that of positively influencing and encouraging other people. It is especially satisfying to coach and to help build people in your own team. My best friend from grade school through high school is still a great source of encouragement for me.

Do I encourage people?

The most important things a leader can accomplish are to have enough strength and enough stature to be able to encourage others. The fundamental quality that enables an individual to keep on learning and growing is courage. Without courage, decisions are not made well, hope is lost, and organizations begin a downward spiral toward failure.

"Whenever you see a successful business, someone once made a courageous decision." Peter Daucher

Someone taking the time, the effort, and the love to encourage me, has initiated some of the greatest times of progress in my life. Leaders often underestimate how powerful their encouragement is to their employees. Do not leave encouragement unsaid, do not neglect regular times of pointing out good things about your employees, and do not take their efforts for granted. Invest time and energy in creatively encouraging your people.

Do I have formal and informal ways of recognizing my employees?

Involve your own employees in developing good recognition programs. The time and resources invested in expressions of appreciation are well spent. Figure out ways to affirm people. Point out when people do things above and beyond the normal call of duty.

I often tell the groups I am consulting or training about how theme parks train killer whales like "Shamu" to do their fantastic performances. The long and short of the story is that the trainer simply points out things that the killer whale does correctly. As the whales are encouraged they start to perform extraordinary tricks and soon a new Shamu is born. These world-class performers only learn their craft by means of recognition for positive performance. You can well imagine that any trainer that is in a tank with a killer whale doesn't want to deliver a message of "Bad whale" to any new killer whale that is being trained. Granted, people are not killer whales. And yes people need to know when they do things wrong. But we need to strengthen the process of recognizing good things in our work place. It is important for employees to hear what they are doing right more often.

Do I really respect people?

I believe that every human being is created in God's image. That doesn't mean I think everyone is delightful, or that I agree with everybody, or any other such fantasy. Nor do I believe that everybody is innately good. What I do believe is that if someone is a human being they are worthy of respect just because of the fact that they are a human being.

I try to have a basic respect for any human being. I may not agree with them, I may hate what they stand for, I certainly don't think murderers should be released from prison. I may not like the way people treat me but I can still have respect for them simply because of this basic belief.

You have to make your own decisions about how you view people. Do you have unconditional respect for other human beings? Do people have to perform a certain way before you respect them?

Do I love my people enough to confront them?

Caring enough about our team to confront them when they are wrong is an important point to reach as a leader. Often, it will take some time and some mutual respect and demonstration of true concern before you can effectively confront someone on your team. We become a powerful team and truly begin to have synergy if we get to the point where we can see "Iron sharpening iron." Also, keep in mind that, to your employees your silence equates to your acceptance. If, while supervising, you notice your employees doing something incorrectly or inappropriately, and you don't take the time to properly confront and counsel them, then they begin to assume that their behavior or performance is acceptable—when, in reality, it is not. As a leader, you *must* take the time to do the appropriate coaching.

The ability to be frank with one another, without destroying friendships and respect, will help rub off the rough spots in our own lives, as well as be of benefit to others in our team. It is the point where we are teachable, and others in our team are teachable. It is that point at which we are sharpening one another.

> **"Others can stop you temporarily; only you can do it permanently."** (Don Ward)

Do I know my team and their dreams and aspirations?

I truly treasure people who have taken the time to listen to my dreams and aspirations. If they then go out of their way to help me in reaching those dreams, then they have earned their place as a life-long friend. As a leader, can you take the time to discover some of the dreams of your people and help them in achieving those dreams?

What do I really believe about people?

What do you believe about the following four statements?

1. Everyone, at least initially, wants to succeed.
2. People do what makes sense to them.
3. Everyone wants to experience personal growth.
4. Everyone wants to make an important difference in life.

In regard to number one, I realize that not everyone does succeed, but it seems that most everyone, as they begin a new job, wants to succeed. Sometimes, after years of disappointment and years of working in a bad system, they just want to get even. But initially, they came to that job and wanted to succeed.

What do you believe about number two? Do people do what makes sense to them? I realize some exhibit bad behavior that actually undermines their success; but, at its core they are probably trying to do something that makes sense to them and that they believe will make the situation better. Granted, it may not accomplish that, but their reasoning (no matter how distorted it might be) still comes from a perspective of doing something good or coping in an effective manner.

Does everyone want to grow? Again, sometimes the weariness of life with its disappointments and burdens prompts people to choose bitterness rather that growth. But initially, most people wanted to experience healthy growth. If someone is not on that road, how can we help him or her rediscover it and regain hope?

Does everyone want to make an important difference? Again, I think most people start off with a sincere desire to make a positive difference. Sometimes things get in the way, or the trail becomes so twisted that they end up harming themselves and the people around them. But the vast majority of people want to make a positive difference in this life. If they are not accomplishing this, at least start with the premise that what they are trying to do is positive and ask questions that will help guide them back to a more successful path.

"The smallest good deed is greater than the greatest intention."

With all the demands put on you as a leader, it is difficult to find time to authentically build people. But it is, perhaps, one of the most enduring activities to which we can dedicate some of our time. It will impact our people as well as our bottom line.

CHAPTER 29
BUILDING TEAMS

As people watch the game of football, they are usually not even conscious of one of the fundamentals of the game. That fundamental is: people with the same color jerseys don't tackle each other!

Suppose you're watching the Super Bowl and suddenly before the snap of the football an offensive guard jumps up, turns around, and viciously sacks his own quarterback. Do you think that would be weird? Most of us would say, "Yes!" It is so unusual it would probably make the evening news. However, in most organizations "tackling" one another is a daily event. Can you remember the last time you were "tackled" at work?

Does your team tackle one another?

One of the first things we can do to build better teamwork is to stop hindering one another. There is plenty of competition, but that competition should remain outside of our organization. We need to compete with others that are vying for our customers. Too often the competition becomes an inner competition. We end up competing with one another even though we are on the same team. We can improve productivity and improve our bottom line simply by stopping the practice of tackling one another.

How much teamwork is in your team?

There are four levels of teamwork. The first level doesn't really involve much working together, and the last one is probably the epitome of working together. Of the four teams listed below, which one best represents the teamwork in your organization?

1. **A bowling team**
2. **A baseball team**
3. **A football team**
4. **A rowing team**

With the bowling team everyone simply adds up his or her own individual scores to create the team effort. There is nothing wrong with bowling teams, but they are actually not much of a team. Each bowler on the team gets up, individually does their part, and then we add up the individual scores. It's a fun time but there is not actually much teamwork involved. We may encourage one another, but that's the extent of the interaction.

A baseball team has more interactions and more teamwork than the bowling team. But even in baseball, if the pitch is thrown, the batter hits the ball and maybe two fielders are involved in fielding the ball and throwing the batter out. In all, there may only be only four or five people involved in any one play. Given the fact that there are eighteen members on each team, that's more interactions than a bowling team—but certainly does not involve the whole team in every play.

The third type of team is like a football team. A football team has eleven people on each side of the ball. In nearly every game, all twenty-two people are involved in some way. Granted, some play more key roles for different plays, but all are involved, nonetheless.

A rowing team is a beautiful thing to watch. There may be as many as eight rowers in one boat. The eight members of the team work in unison, all are agreed on the direction in which they will row, and they all row in synchronized unity. The result is a highly functional team. A rowing team is one of the best examples of synergy. The rest of the team actually multiplies the efforts of each individual. The eight individuals on the rowing team can row faster than any one of them could in their own individual boats.

So, at what level of teamwork does your team operate? Is there any way to take it to the next level? What training and encouragement will be needed to get your team to truly be synergistic? Synergy is where we can take two plus two, and it equals six or seven. Great teams are fun to work in, and are great ways to serve our customers.

Does everyone on your team know they are vitally important?

Many years ago, I memorized a short poem that illustrates the importance of everyone on a team. Even those members on your team that seem insignificant are vital to its success. The poem is entitled:

For the Want of a Nail

For the want of a nail, a shoe was lost, for the want of a shoe, a horse was lost, for the want of a horse a rider was lost, for the want of a rider a battle was lost, for the want of a battle, the war was lost—all for the want of a nail!
(Author unknown)

Maybe someone on your team is like that nail. If they don't know how vital they are to the whole operation, they sometimes will not do a quality job. That lack of quality can end up costing us all success. Be sure to communicate in many different ways how vital each member is to the success of the whole team.

Is your team set up for success?

I have found it essential to have the team set up for success. Some teams fail because they were not properly formed.

Some things to think about in forming your team are pointed out in the following questions,

> Does your team have a strong advocate in top leadership?
> Do you have a designated team leader?
> Does your team have a team scribe?(someone who takes notes and keeps us on track by way of documentation)
> Does your team have a clear way of making conclusive decisions?
> Does your team make decisions based on good data?
> Does your team focus on the customer?
> Does your team know the parameters and the fiscal responsibility they have?

Does your team have a clear purpose?

Does your team know to whom it is accountable?

Does your team have a clear method for follow through?

Does your team study the results of their decisions?

Does your team have a clear way of engrafting their improvements into the current system?

Does your team have a clear way of recognizing the contributions of its members?

Do we have mutual respect for each other?

One of the most important traits of a great team is mutual respect among the team members. Mutual respect doesn't mean we love everybody else on the team. It does require that we have respect for everyone on the team, and for the important function that each one plays on the team. Mutual respect will enable us to work together and succeed together. Individual team members stand together and support one another.

CHAPTER 30
CHARACTER

A person's character is made up of the total depth and quality of that person's behavior. Habits of thought, actions, attitudes, and one's own personal philosophy of life reveal character. The foundation and fundamentals of our character are most often revealed during crisis. It is the pressure of life that reveals character. Any of us can feign great character when things are going well. It is when our backs are against the wall, and there is the potential for great loss, that character is revealed.

As these words are being penned, the headlines in newspapers across the nation are filled with examples of corporate fraud and politicians ready to use it for whatever political advantage they can engineer. Obviously, leaders have always needed to foster good character. I have found good character takes a lot of inner strength. It also takes a wealth of insight and a clear view of the big picture.

Short cuts always look inviting. The problem with short cuts is that they put our character at great risk. Too often present gains result in long term shame. Every leader has the temptation to accept the lie that he/she will be the one to escape any repercussions for wrongdoing. The real question is: do we really believe the Old Testament verse that states, "Be sure your sin will find you out?" (Numbers 32:23)

What shape is my character in?

In chapter three, we talked about the importance of image. Those things concerning our image are important. In this last chapter, we are talking about character. Character involves things within us that perhaps only we know about, but will prove to encourage us, nonetheless. They will aid us, or when the pressure is on, will prove to undo us.

"A gentleman is one who considers the rights of others before his own feelings, and the feelings of others before his own rights...You should care more about your character than your reputation. Your character is what you really are, your reputation is only what people think about you." (John Wooden, *They call me coach*)

What are the habits of my thought life?

In my inner being, what do I habitually find myself pondering? What is my true philosophy of life?

All of us are constantly talking to ourselves. This is that voice in the back of our minds that is reviewing and rehearsing the very core of our thoughts. What do you talk to yourself about? Are your thoughts positive for the most part? Is the habit of your inner thought based on things that are noble, things that are above board and of good report?

I know of no human being that has perfect character. Good character is a habit, not a perfected science. People who habitually demonstrate good character will be long lasting and will endure.

"Fame is a vapor, popularity an accident, riches take wing, and only character endures." (Charles R. Swindol, *Hope Again*)

Do I keep my promises and my commitments?

Sometimes it is impossible to keep all commitments. Things will come up that we had no way of anticipating. But, is it your habit to endure personal hardship or inconvenience to keep promises and deadlines?

Is my character tempered with mercy?

Endurance and high character are of extreme value to the leader. All of us need to have an attitude of grace. Grace is that unmerited favor that we extend to our fellow human beings. It should also be extended to ourselves on many occasions. None of us is perfect, and no one around us will perform perfectly. Hopefully, a part of our personal philosophy is a belief in forgiveness. Often we will have to choose between holding an offense and becoming bitter, or letting go of an offense by way of forgiveness. Isn't it better to free ourselves of negativity through forgiveness rather than expending unnecessary personal energy by holding a grudge?

"Life is a grindstone. Whether it grinds you down or polishes you up depends on what you are made of." (James S Hewett, *Illustrations Unlimited*)

The End

Contact Information

To contact Stan Jensen Ph.D.

To find out more information about
Dr. Stan Jensen's Speaking, Consulting,
Training, Personal Coaching, and Writing

Contact Stan Jensen
Phone: 515.963.8026
Fax: 515.965.2833
Dr_Stan_Jensen@msn.com

Leadership Enterprises, Inc.
9035 NE 46th Street
Bondurant, Iowa 50035